The Business of Murder

A Play

Richard Harris

GW00394056

Samuel French - London
New York - Toronto - Hollywood

THE BUSINESS OF MURDER

First presented at the Theatre Royal, Windsor, in association with David Gordon Productions on 10th February 1981, with the following cast of characters:

Hallett	George Sewell
Stone	Francis Matthews
Dee	Lynette Davis

The play directed by Hugh Goldie

Designed by John Page

Subsequently presented by Bill Kenwright in association with the Windsor Theatre Company at the Duchess Theatre, London, on 2nd April 1981, with the same cast of characters, director and designer.

The action takes place in a first-floor flat

ACT I   Scene 1   An autumn afternoon at about 3.30 p.m.
              Scene 2   Just before 8 p.m. the same evening

ACT II   A few moments later

Time—the present

ACT I

Scene 1

A first-floor flat in a converted house in the inner London suburbs. About 3.30 p.m. on an autumn afternoon

The sitting-room is separated from the front door by a small lobby, the front door being angled so that it is only visible when open. The lobby is shaped and angled by the well of the stairs leading to the floor above. Under this stairwell is a low junk cupboard. Next to the front door and therefore out of sight are some coathooks and a second door, which is presumed to lead to the bathroom

Below the lobby is the door to the bedroom, which is simply furnished with a single bed, a wardrobe and a chest of drawers. This is a scrim set, the interior being visible only when illuminated

On the opposite side, the upstage corner of the room has been professionally partitioned off to form a small kitchen. The entrance to the kitchen has no door so that the interior is visible at all times. A sink unit, a fridge, a cooker and a pedal bin can be seen. There is a venetian blind at the kitchen window

The sitting-room is furnished with a three-piece suite, a coffee table and a nest of small tables. DR *there is a television set, and* UL *by the entrance to the kitchen there is a table and a standard lamp. There is a large sash window in the centre of the back wall. Beneath the window there is a small desk with drawers and an upright chair. There are bookshelves next to the window. There is nothing grand about the place: neither is it seedy. All in all, it is typical of the sort of part-furnished accommodation rented by professional couples who are respectable but not wealthy*

When the Curtain *rises, the room, usually very tidy, is in something of a mess. The cushions on the settee are disarranged as though someone has been lying full-length. On the coffee table before the settee are a tray bearing the remains of an egg and bacon meal, two empty cans of beer, an empty and crumpled cigarette packet and a breadboard holding the remains of a loaf and a carving knife. On the floor near the table are a filthy ashtray, a newspaper, a discarded telephone directory and the telephone, which has been moved there on its trailing lead from the desk. The television set is turned on and the low sound of a racing commentary can be heard. The bedroom is not illuminated*

Hallett stands in the centre of the room. He is in his early 40s. He has goodish looks going a little puffy round the eyes through too many long sessions with too many short drinks. He has a deceptively casual manner most of the time, but has a short fuse and doesn't suffer those he considers to be fools gladly. He wears a hat and a light-coloured raincoat—one of those mass-produced Korean copies of a Burberry. Beneath the coat he wears a grey suit, plain

*blue shirt and tie. He takes off his hat and flips it on to a chair. He is used to
entering other people's homes and putting himself at ease. His coat is open and
he thrusts his hands into his trouser pockets to jiggle the coins there—a habit
he has when weighing up situations—as his eyes unhurriedly, efficiently, take
in the room. His eyes are drawn to the television, and he starts to take off his
coat*

*Stone comes out of the bedroom, closing the door behind him. He is about the
same age and build as Hallett but seems a much less positive man. He is rather
nondescript and wears glasses. A humourless, rather prissy man. He wears a
dark raglan raincoat over an oldish but well-preserved suit. He gives a hopeless
little gesture and speaks as though he can't believe it*

Stone He isn't here.

*Hallett pauses in taking off his coat, but decides to shed it anyway and tosses it
carelessly down by his hat*

Hallett How long did you say we'd be?
Stone Sorry?
Hallett (*patiently*) When you phoned him, how long did you say we'd be?

*Hallett looks at the television. Stone frowns and then speaks carefully—as
though having difficulty in putting his thoughts together, his eyes also being
drawn to the television*

Stone I said we were coming straight round. I said you understood the
situation and ... (*With a sudden flash of irritation*) What's he playing at
for God's sake? Either he wants me to help him or... (*His irritation
becomes anger*) Look at this mess. (*He turns off the television, scoops up the
telephone directory and puts it on the sofa, and takes up the newspaper,
folding it neatly*)
Hallett Par for the course nowadays.
Stone Sorry?
Hallett Kids. Teenagers.
Stone Would *your* son carry on like this?
Hallett Haven't got one. Haven't got any. (*With a flat smile*) Never found
the need. Got a dog, though. (*He moves to glance down from the window,
but turns, and with his flat smile*) Insanity is hereditary: you get it from
your kids.

Stone looks at him. Then realizes it's meant to be a joke

Stone Oh. Yes. (*He manages the flutter of a smile*)

Hallett looks around, jiggling coins

   Look. I'm very sorry.
Hallett Perhaps he just went out for some fags.
Stone He had no right going anywhere. (*He puts the newspaper on the arm of
the sofa*)
Hallett (*moving to pick up the empty cigarette packet*) Possible though. (*He

lets the packet fall back on to the table and moves away to glance into the kitchen)

Stone, clearly for something to do, puts the beer cans and packet on to the tray. Hearing the noise, Hallett turns and watches expressionlessly as Stone takes up the tray with one hand and bends to take up the breadboard with the other. As he does, the carving knife falls from it on to the floor. He dithers slightly and Hallett takes up the knife by the handle and puts it on the tray for him HALLETT: OO! WOOPSA DAISY!

Stone Thanks. Thank you. (*He takes the things into the kitchen and deposits them*)

Hallett takes out a packet of thin cigars. Stone returns and Hallett offers the packet to him but just as quickly remembers

Hallett No, you don't, do you. I gave it up once. Came to the conclusion it was only the tar that was holding me together.

Again the flat smile and again the joke, for what it was worth, are lost on Stone. Hallett lights his cigar as Stone starts tidying the cushions

   Do me a favour, eh?
Stone Sorry?
Hallett Relax.
Stone I know it's ridiculous but I—I just don't seem able to cope.
Hallett I'll cope. It's my job. Just the one bedroom is it?
Stone Umm—yes.
Hallett You don't mind if I have a quick shufti. (*He moves towards the bedroom and opens the door*)
Stone (*taking a few nervous steps after him*) Well I mean, is that really necessary?

Hallett looks quickly inside the bedroom with his expert eye, but sounds casual as he speaks

Hallett I like your curtains.
Stone (*tetchily*) Do you?
Hallett Oh yes, very *House and Garden*, very Henry Cooper. (*He moves away from the bedroom, smiling amiably*)
Stone I did say he wasn't here.
Hallett So it's just the bedroom, the kitchen ...
Stone And the bathroom. Quite an unusual combination wouldn't you say?
Hallett The bathroom being ...
Stone ~~Just inside the door.~~ (*He makes a polite, open-handed gesture in the direction of the lobby*) THROUGH THE BEDROOM OR UP THROUGH THE LOBBY.

Hallett remains unperturbed at Stone's clear irritation

Hallett (*moving towards the lobby*) I'll bet you've got blue water.

   Hallett exits R

Stone stands for a moment, then moves to carefully close the bedroom door. A moment. Then he moves towards the lobby

Stone Look—perhaps I should telephone you or something.
Hallett (*off*) Give it ten minutes. Now I'm here.
Stone Or perhaps I should just let him get on with it.

Hallett enters

Hallett No rush. Not for me. How about you?
Stone No, I—I've taken the afternoon off.

Hallett sits casually in an armchair. Stone, taking the cue, sits edgily on the sofa

Hallett I was wrong about the water, wasn't I?
Stone Perhaps next time you come.

Hallett smiles. A moment

Hallett Live on your own, do you?
Stone Since my wife died. We had a house, but ... Well, when Clive—my son—decided to go off and "do his own thing" ... there didn't really seem much point. (*He frowns, as though suppressing some painful memory but snaps out of it with an attempt at conversation*) You're married, are you?
Hallett Fifteen years next month.
Stone It's a—it's a good marriage then, is it? I mean ... (*He gives an awkward little smile, aware of the gaucheness of his remark*)
Hallett We're very lucky. We've got a lot in common. We were both married on the same day. (*A moment. Then with a change of tone*) She puts up with me: man can't ask for much more, can he?
Stone I've often thought—it must be very difficult, married to a policeman.
Hallett Yeah, I wouldn't try it if I were you.
Stone It's a very—demanding job, isn't it? Policework? I suppose if you're a really good policeman it becomes—well—obsessive. I understand that the divorce rate is very high.
Hallett Do you?
Stone (*swept along by a sudden enthusiasm*) I suppose it's all those—unsocial hours you have to work. Shift work, isn't it? Sometimes all night. (*He allows himself a smile at a naughty thought*) Although I suppose ... No, that's very rude of me.
Hallett (*irritated, but maintaining an all-boys-together* bonhomie) Come on now, let's have it.
Stone No, I shouldn't have, it's—well, it could be construed as offensive.
Hallett I couldn't construe anything, Mr Stone, I'm not educated enough.
Stone Well ... what I meant was ... if you were a bit of a ladies' man—I mean not you, I mean someone in your job—well, being out all night and presumably not having to strictly account for your movements—well—I'm sure you know what I mean.
Hallett Naughties on night-duty.
Stone Well ... yes. (*Again he tries a smile*)
Hallett 'S why most of us are in the job, Mr Stone ... plenty of fresh air, nice little pension and ample opportunity to get your leg over. (*He leans forward to take up the ashtray*)

Stone (*quickly on his feet and taking the ashtray*) I'll just empty it.
Hallett Don't bother on my account.
Stone No, please, I can't stand this sort of filth, really. (*He takes the ashtray into the kitchen and empties it into the bin*)

Hallett gives a sardonic little jerk of the head and scratches the side of his neck, thinking what a berk this man Stone is

Hallett (*calling*) Did he bring anything with him?
Stone (*entering from the kitchen*) Sorry?
Hallett Your son. When he suddenly—descended on you last night. Did he bring anything?
Stone (*crossing to put the ashtray at Hallett's elbow*) No. (*But, uncertainly*) Well ... yes.

Hallett looks at him, waiting for him to go on. Stone moves across to the junk cupboard, bends down and opens the door. Just inside—and virtually filling the doorway—is a battered old railway trunk with a shiny new padlock on its hasp

He brought this.
Hallett (*unhurriedly moving across to the cupboard*) Came on his bike then, did he?
Stone That's a point. (*He frowns*) I suppose someone must have given him a lift. (*He stares at the trunk*) I didn't think to ask: it was all so—confusing at the time.
Hallett (*prodding the trunk with a foot*) Heavy is it?
Stone (*frowning*) I've no idea.
Hallett You didn't help him up the stairs. with it.
Stone No. (*Suddenly irritated*) I said. He telephoned, I told him I had to go out and arranged to leave the key.
Hallett Under the mat.
Stone Well ... yes.
Hallett No wonder you people get burgled.

Stone grasps one of the handles and lifts that end of the trunk, pulling it partly out into the lobby

Stone Not that heavy. Try it.
Hallett Bad back. (*With a change of tone*) He didn't happen to mention what was in it?
Stone Well yes. Books and things.
Hallett "Things."
Stone (*making an impotent gesture*) His things, all his things.
Hallett Nice new padlock. Wonder if it works?

Stone looks at him, then pulls on the padlock which is clearly fastened

Stone You ... you think we should open it.
Hallett Waddaya think we'll find? (*He offers his big flat smile*)
Stone (*insisting*) Do you want me to open it?
Hallett Not our property, is it? Mind you, we could always say we smelled gas.

Stone (*looking around*) I suppose there must be something I could use ..

Hallett Leave it.

Stone I thought you ...

Hallett Let *him* do it. Eh? (*He moves to sit in the chair*) And you've no idea where he's been living?

Stone (*after a slight pause*) He wouldn't say. (*He manages a smile*) Wonderful relationship, isn't it, when a son won't tell his own father where he's living. (*He sits, uneasily*) I suppose you see this sort of mess every day of your life.

Hallett (*shrugging*) There's a lot of it about.

Stone You bring them up the best way you know how ... But that's just it, isn't it? It doesn't seem to matter what you do ... It's got nothing to do with class or environment or—or anything. Every time you open a paper there's some kid either taking drugs or pushing drugs or—or dying of drugs. You think—when you do think, because this sort of thing only happens to other people—you think ... Where did it all start? Where's the need? And then your own son comes home and hits you right between the eyes with it.

Hallett If they couldn't get the stuff they wouldn't use it. Money. That's where it starts, Mr Stone. Big business.

Stone It's not as simple as that, surely?

Hallett (*crushing out his cigar with a sudden irritable movement*) I'm not a psychiatrist—or a ~~welfare~~ worker bless their little hearts—I'm a copper. You break the law, I feel your collar—yeah, it's as simple as that. Use your phone? (*He bends to take up the telephone and places it on his lap to dial*)

Stone Umm ... please.

Hallett (*dialling*) Just let 'em know I'm still alive.

Stone (*standing, concerned*) You won't say anything, I mean, we did promise him there'd be no names at this stage ...

Hallett Scouts' Honour. (*Immediately speaking into the receiver*) Hello love, Superintendent Hallet, gimmee the C.I.D. Room, will you? (*He cups the receiver*) You're an informant, Mr Stone. At the minute, it's strictly you and me. (*He uncups the receiver*) Try and sound a *bit* efficient, will you, I could've been a punter.... Oh, I see, you were pre-occupied, were you? (*He winks at Stone*) What is it, *Playboy* or fiddling your expenses?

Stone becomes aware that he is still in his raincoat. He takes it off and makes to move to the lobby, then turns and takes up Hallett's hat and coat. He exits R to hang up both coats and the hat in the lobby

Anything happened? ... Oh is he? Well tell him from me to go easy, I don't want any more aggravation. (*He looks at his watch*) I'm popping over the courts for half an hour, should be back around five. Oh, yeah, and you can tell Ritchie I want to see him. Right. (*He replaces the receiver, puts the telephone back on the floor*)

Stone enters

Stone (*trying to make a sort of joke out of it*) So that's what I'm called is it— an informant.

Hallett Information, Mr Stone—it's our bread and butter.

Stone A grass.

Hallett Watch a lot of television, do you?

Stone Well, no, not really, I ...

Hallett All the cops and robbers shows, do you?

Stone Well, no, I ...

Hallett You know all about "grasses", you know all about our sex-lives ...Course you do. (*He smiles, but now there is an edge*) What about that clown on the BBC, eh? Detective-Superintendent? More like a ladies' bloody hairdresser. Still. He always gets his man, doesn't he? Gotta be good for the image. (*Again the smile*) Know where it comes from, Mr Stone?

Stone Sorry?

Hallett "Grass." The word "grass".

Stone Umm ... snake, is that it? Snake in the grass?

Hallett The old Ink Spots' number. *Whispering Grass.* (*He puts a hand to his mouth*) Whisper, whisper, whisper. (*He shrugs, grins flatly*) Whispering Grass.

Stone Even so ... it's an ugly word. Even uglier when applied to a father informing on his own son.

Hallett D'you want to help him or don't you? (*Suddenly overcome by his irritation, he gets up and moves to look down from the window*)

Stone I'm sorry.

Hallett We're all sorry.

A slight pause

Stone I see.

Hallett Do you, do you really.

A slight pause

Stone I think perhaps I should telephone you.

Hallett Second thoughts?

Stone Not at all.

Hallett You've shown the dog the bone. Can't take it back. (*With his smile*) Won't let you.

Stone Nevertheless, I would have thought ...

Hallett Would've thought what?

Stone A little more understanding perhaps.

Hallett I'm an arrogant pig, Mr Stone. It's how I get through my day.

Stone I'm not used to this sort of thing. You obviously are.

Hallett turns to look at him. A moment

Hallett You're absolutely right. Now it's my turn to say sorry. Thing is ... I get tired. (*With his flat smile*) Tired of breaking down lavatory doors and finding seventeen-year-old kids groping for a vein and squatting in their own vomit and then coming to nice clean houses like this and making all the right noises because, worried though we might be, we mustn't let the neighbours know, must we, we must keep it respectable.

Stone Is this your shock treatment, Mr Hallett? Your—set speech—pre-

pared to galvanize the likes of me into oiling the wheels of your particular
profession?

Hallett looks at him. Then grins slowly

Hallett Could be. (*A moment. Then with a change of tone*) Last night your
son turns up on your doorstep, frightened out of his wick. He tells you
he's been pushing the stuff, he's cheated on the heavy brigade and they're
after his blood. He's frightened bad enough to want to name names. He
trusts you and he's heard that he can trust me. You and I arrange a meet
and just like everyone else, you want it on the q.t., that's fine, that's OK,
you want confidence, this stage of the game you can have it. So we have
our meet—in the middle of Wimbledon Common. I would have preferred
a large Scotch in a warm boozer m'self, but *you* watch television, *you*
know how these things are done. You phone him here, tell him I'm
prepared to play ball, persuade him it's all right for me to come round and
talk business. We come round and he's gone—now—does anyone else
know he's been here?

Stone No. He was—absolutely insistent on that.

Hallett So. He's been using the phone—right? (*He points to the phone on the
floor*)

Stone Umm ... yes ... it, it certainly ...

Hallett So if no-one phoned *him*, chances are he phoned somebody. And
maybe because of what was said he had it away on his heels again. Or ...
or somebody *did* know he came here—somebody who helped him with
that thing—(*he points to the trunk*)—and then put the frighteners on him.
Now you're absolutely sure you don't know where he could have gone,
who any of his friends are?

A moment. And Stone shakes his head

Stone Nothing. (*He sits on the arm of the sofa, moving the newspaper to do so*)

Hallett Then we'll just have to wait and hope he makes contact.

Stone Just a minute ... (*He takes up the newspaper, turning it to point to a
margin*) There's a telephone number.

Hallett (*looking*) Is it his writing?

Stone It's not mine, I suppose it must be.

Hallett Try it.

Stone (*looking at him*) What shall I say?

Hallett Just see who answers then hang up.

*A moment. Then Stone checks the number on the paper, takes up the telephone
and puts it back on the desk where it belongs. As he dials, Hallett takes up the
newspaper to idly flip through it*

Stone Is that three-four or eight-four?

Hallett (*looking*) Three-four.

Stone continues dialling. A moment. Then he cups the receiver

Stone (*puzzled*) It's a cinema.

Hallett stabs a finger, indicating for him to hang up

(*Uncupping the receiver*) I'm so sorry, wrong number. (*He hangs up and moves away, taking a handkerchief from his pocket to dab his hands*)

The telephone rings. *Stone looks from it to Hallett. A moment. Then Stone takes up the receiver*

(*On the phone*) Nine-three-two-nine ... (*A moment, then he cups the receiver*) It's him, he's in a call-box ... (*He uncups the receiver and, unable to keep the concern from his voice*) Where are you, for God's sake? ... Yes, he's here and I want you to talk to him. ... *Why?* Look, just—just talk to him, will you? ... Now, wait a minute, Clive. ... Clive? (*But the caller has obviously rung off. Stone slowly lowers the receiver. A moment*) He said he—just wanted to get out. He's seeing someone and then he'll—he'll be here tonight. At about eight o'clock. Definitely. He said he's ... He said he's very sorry.

A moment. Hallett jiggles his money

Hallett You took my coat.
Stone What? Oh—yes—sorry.

Stone exits R *and enters again almost immediately, carrying Hallett's hat and coat, which he gives to him*

Hallett You won't be going out, will you?
Stone Well, no, I ...
Hallett Better if you stay in, eh? He might be early. Soon as he shows up, gimmee a ring.
Stone And if he doesn't?
Hallett (*shrugging*) We'll find him. Better if he co-operates, that's all. He could put me into a big one and I'd like that. Get me picture in the paper again. (*With his flat smile, he moves to the door*)
Stone It's just that ...

Hallett stops

It's just that he's very frightened.
Hallett He's got cause to be, Mr Stone. ~~My life.~~ He's got cause to be .

A moment. Then Hallett exits R. *We see the door open and close behind him*

Stone stands quite still for a moment, and then moves to the window. He looks down carefully, watching Hallett move away. Stone turns away from the window. He looks suddenly relieved of a great strain. He has a hand to his stomach as though he might vomit from the sheer release of tension. But now he pulls himself together and goes through what is a set of clearly rehearsed movements. He takes from his pocket a folded typewritten sheet which he unfolds and places on the backrest of the desk. He refers briefly to this checklist then moves to the desk, takes out a pair of thin gloves, puts them on. As he does, he again refers to his checklist. He drags the trunk a little further into the room, takes out a set of keys, unlocks the padlock. From inside the trunk he takes out a nondescript holdall, a raincoat and a hat. The clothing is identical to that worn by Hallett. He puts the hat and coat over the back of the sofa, closes the trunk, places the holdall on top of it and from the holdall takes out a black plastic bin-bag which he opens and places on top of the trunk. He returns to look at his checklist, then moves into the kitchen, takes a vacuum flask from the fridge and comes out to stand it carefully on the sofa by the clothing. He returns to the kitchen, takes two plastic freezer bags from a drawer. He then— by the tip of its blade—takes up the carving knife he dropped earlier and moves out into the sitting-room, carefully sliding the knife handle-first into one of the bags. He gently places the wrapped bag on to the bin-bag. He takes the second bag to the ashtray and tips Hallett's cigar butt into it and takes it back to the trunk. In doing so, he glances towards the lobby which gives him a sudden pleasing reminder

Ah yes ... the button ... (*He dips into a pocket to take out a coat button which he holds up to admire with a sarcastic*) Not often we get a bonus— thankyousomuch, Superintendent.

He rubs the button between gloved thumb and finger, puts the button into the bag with the cigar-butt, wraps the bin-bag around the two plastic bags and neatly places them inside the holdall. He takes up the vacuum flask and stands it carefully inside the holdall. He goes to the desk, opens a drawer, takes out a bundle of papers, puts them inside the holdall. He folds the raincoat neatly and places it inside the holdall. He takes up the hat, brushing it, and places that inside the holdall. He stands for a moment, making a mental check of the contents of the holdall, then—satisfied—zips it shut. He returns to his checklist, then moves to the telephone, mouthing a number, and dials. When he speaks into the phone, he is briskly efficient with a slightly more up-market accent than his usual one

Good afternoon, is it possible to speak to Miss Redmond or has the meeting already started? ... Miss Dee Redmond? ... Oh it has. ... No, no, don't disturb her, I'll phone her later at home. Thankyousomuch. (*He replaces the receiver quickly before any questions can be asked. After a moment, he takes up the receiver and dials another number. As he speaks, he carries the telephone to the sofa and sits down*) Put me through to the duty officer, will you? (*A moment and now quickly, agitated*) Who is this? ... Ah yes—I want to make a complaint. My wife has just telephoned me here at my office. ... Burroughs, Mr Burroughs. ... No, just listen to what I have to say, *please*. ... She has been unable to move her car all afternoon because someone who has no right to be there has parked right across the front of her. Now we pay a great deal of money to live in these flats and this is a private forecourt—it's clearly marked—and I want something done about it. ... Endersby Court. The car is a ~~Cortina~~, a green Cortina registration number ~~VGH-five-seven-four-R~~ (*As he speaks, he checks this number against his list*) If you check your records you'll find that this isn't the first complaint to be made about this man whoever he is. ... I see. ... Well, I repeat, this is private property and if it happens again I shall expect some kind of action. (*He replaces the receiver sharply. He looks at his list, then, satisfied, screws the paper into a ball, puts it in the ashtray and, taking a lighter from his pocket, sets fire to it. As it burns, he tears the telephone number from the newspaper, screws it up and puts it into the ashtray to burn. He returns the telephone to the desk and moves towards the lobby*)

STATION STAGE CREW AT FRONT DOOR !!

He exits R and returns almost immediately, pulling on his raincoat

He takes up the ashtray, carries it into the kitchen, puts it in the sink and turns the tap on it. He lets it run as he buttons up his coat, then turns off the tap. He moves out of the kitchen switching off the light, then takes up the holdall and looks finally round the room. He switches off the sitting-room light

He exits R, closing the door gently behind him

The Lights slowly fade to a Black-out

SCENE 2

The same. Just before 8 p.m.

When the Lights come up, the room is much tidier and looks far more homely. The window curtains are drawn and some of the side lights are on. There is general evidence, perhaps, of a woman's touch. A bowl of flowers is set on the table by the kitchen, next to some glasses and bottles of drink. Some knitting and needles are lying on one of the armchairs, and there is a pile of French's Acting Editions on the coffee table. A small portable typewriter rests under its cover on the desk. Stone's suit jacket hangs over the back of the sofa. The television set is on, the sound turned low. The trunk is now placed more centrally, and its lid is open, raised towards the audience

Stone is just straightening up from the trunk. He is wearing a comfortable cardigan with the sleeves pushed back showing bare forearms. He is wearing thin rubber gloves which are stained with blood. He snaps off the gloves and folds them into a plastic bag. He puts the bag into the pocket of his jacket and then hangs the jacket neatly over the desk chair. He rubs his fingers together in prim distaste and goes into the kitchen to wash his hands in water already in the sink. On the draining-board is a small pile of freshly washed crockery—place settings for two—and the upturned vacuum flask. He pulls out the plug, wipes his hands meticulously on a tea-towel as he crosses to peer down carefully from the window. He pulls a watch from his pocket, glances at it and straps it on to his wrist as he returns the tea-towel to the kitchen. He comes out to survey the room critically, mentally running through his checklist. He reaches into a pocket and pulls out a handkerchief from which he turns out a key. He puts the key under a vase on the bookshelves and returns the handkerchief to his pocket. He moves to the bedroom, opens the door and leans in. He remains in the doorway, looking down at the (unseen) bed for a moment, then closes the door and moves to look down into the trunk as he rolls down his sleeves. He closes the trunk lid, snaps the padlock shut. He crosses to the drinks table, checks the glasses, then turns on the standard lamp next to the table. He moves to sit on the sofa, taking up a glass of sherry from the coffee table. He sips it. He takes up the top copy of the books, opens it at a random page and places it face down as though it were in the process of being read. He sits, his eyes drawn to the television. But then he gets up and moves to look from the window. A moment. And suddenly he is reacting. He pulls the curtains tighter, takes up the telephone and dials

Stone (*after a moment*) Mr Hallett please. (*After a pause*) Mr Hallett? Mr
Stone. You'll remember ... (*As though afraid of being overheard*) My son
has just arrived. ... Yes. ... Yes, I will. (*He replaces the receiver and stands
a moment, tensely*)

*The doorbell rings. Stone rubs hands which have begun to sweat down his
trousers. Clearly he is steeling himself. He turns on the light in the lobby*

Finally settling his nerves, he goes off to open the front door

(*Off; brightly*) Miss Redmond.
Dee (*off*) Mr Stone?
Stone (*off*) Do come in, please.

*Stone enters, followed by Dee. She is an attractive woman in her late 20s.
She is capable and bright but there's an underlying nervous edge about her.
She is wearing casual but expensive clothing, carries a shoulder-bag and an
A4-size envelope, addressed, stamped and open*

(*As he enters*) You found us all right then.
Dee More or less.
Stone Sorry?
Dee (*smiling*) You didn't mention the one-way system.

He looks at her for a moment and then suddenly realizes and is all apologies

Stone You're absolutely right, I completely forgot. They've only just done
it, you see.
Dee (*still pleasantly*) It doesn't matter—really.
Stone I'm normally so good with directions.
Dee Anyway—here I am.
Stone Yes. Here you are. And very nice of you to spare us the time. (*He
smiles at her*)

Dee finds herself smiling back at him

(*Breaking the moment*) Do sit down—please. (*He indicates the armchair* R,
then realizes the knitting is there and moves it to the nest of tables)

*Dee sits down, putting her bag down by the side of the chair and the envelope
on the arm of the chair. Stone switches off the television*

I'll just tell my wife you're here and then I'll get you a drink.
Dee That would be nice—thank you.

He makes to move into the bedroom but bends towards her

Stone (*quietly*) She—er—she wanted to have a rest before you came. She
gets so tired, I'm afraid.

*Dee nods sympathetically. Again he makes to go and she bends down for her
bag, but again he leans close to her*

If I can just say, Miss Redmond ...
Dee Dee—please.

Stone (*smiling shyly*) If I can just say ... I know you're extremely busy and
—well—I really am very grateful. (*He moves to the bedroom door. As he
opens the door; quietly*) Helen darling ... Miss Redmond is here ...

He exits into the bedroom, closing the door quietly behind him

*Left alone, Dee heaves a sigh and takes out a packet of cigarettes and a lighter
from her bag, gets up, looks around the room, and is just about to light a
cigarette when she notices the pile of books and is about to look more closely at
them*

    *Stone enters, quietly closing the bedroom door behind him. He sort of flaps
his arms in an embarrassed way*

I'm afraid she's fallen asleep.
Dee Oh. (*She looks at her cigarette, unsure now whether or not to light it*)
Stone It's these new pills they're giving her. It's supposed to be four a day
but I'm sure she takes more. The only way to find out I suppose is to
count them but ... I don't know. What do you do when someone's ...
(*With an obvious effort to be bright*) Anyway, she'll be out in a minute,
bright as a button I promise you. Now then ... what can I offer you to
drink?
Dee You're sure it wouldn't be better if I just ...
Stone Please. She's so looking forward to meeting you. It'll give her such a
lift. (*Before she can protest, he takes up his sherry glass and crosses to the
drinks table*) Now then ... let me see if I can guess ... (*He waves a waggish
finger at her*) Vodka and tonic.
Dee (*lighting her cigarette*) How very clever.
Stone (*pleased with himself*) A slice of lemon and lots of ice—yes?
Dee You've been following me.
Stone You've discovered my little secret—foiled again!

*She sits in the armchair R, as he pours out two drinks into somewhat inappro-
priately small glasses. He pours them, holding the glass at eye level, as though
the process were extremely critical*

Actually ... I'm rather good with drinks. You know. Guessing.
Dee How about food?
Stone Food. No. But I'll hazard a guess and say you don't eat regularly
enough.
Dee Ah—now I understand—you've been talking to my mother.
Stone Working girls—you're all the same. I've seen the way you hoard your
luncheon vouchers. (*He goes into the kitchen to take ice from a bowl in the
fridge*)
Dee That takes me back a bit.
Stone (*returning*) Sorry?
Dee Luncheon vouchers.
Stone You're hardly old enough, surely?
Dee Oh, I'm old enough, believe me. Particularly today I'm old enough.
Stone My first job, I remember ... Four pounds a week plus luncheon

vouchers. Half a crown a day. Twelve and a half p. Mind you ... in those
days ... Cheers.

*They drink—and he realizes that she doesn't have an ashtray. He places a
small table from the nest beside her and puts an ashtray on it, so that he is
bending close to her as he speaks*

They did your car all right then.

Dee (*slightly puzzled*) Er ... yes, yes they did.

Stone You mentioned it was going in for a service today. When I phoned.

Dee Did I?

Stone I thought you might have had to come on the tube.

Dee No. (*With a change of tone*) I came straight from town actually.

Stone That's right, you had to go to a meeting. A "script conference" I
think you said.

Dee Yes. (*She smiles, but is still faintly puzzled*)

Stone (*moving to sit on the sofa*) I must say we enjoyed your last television
play enormously.

Dee Thank you.

Stone There was a very good write-up in the *Telegraph*.

Dee Yes, it—er—it seems to have gone down very well.

Stone Very good acting, I thought.

Dee Yes, I was very lucky.

A slight pause

Stone We saw your very first play, you know.

Dee Ah.

Stone Excellent.

Dee Thank you.

Stone It was very—real. Documentary almost.

A slight pause

Dee It was actually based on something I was involved in.

Stone (*impressed*) You actually knew those people.

She nods

Well I never.

Dee When I say I knew them, that isn't quite true. Knew of them. I was a
newspaper reporter in the town where it happened.

Stone And it sort of—stuck in your mind.

Dee Fascinated me, I suppose.

Stone Would that be because of your—what shall I say—compassion for
the people involved, or because you saw it as a good story?

Dee Both. (*She flicks ash into the ashtray with a sudden rather nervous little
movement*)

Stone And that was the start of all your success.

Dee (*smiling*) Depends what you mean by success.

Stone But you do very well—we see your name on television all the time.

Dee Ah! That's success, is it?

Stone (*ploughing on*) Plays, police series—everything. That's really what prompted Helen—my wife—to send her little story to you. You being a woman and writing the sort of thing she would like to write. It must be very gratifying to know that you have succeeded where so many others have failed.

Dee (*patently insincere*) Yes, I've been awfully lucky.

Stone Luck. Yes. Luck *does* enter into so many things, doesn't it? I mean, take yourself for example ... For all your undoubted hard work, your ...

Dee We're all dealt a few good cards in our time—it's whether we have the ability to take advantage of them—wouldn't you agree?

Stone Oh indeed, indeed I do. And please don't misunderstand me. But the fact does remain that had you not met those unfortunate people some, what, six years ago, you might still be working on a local newspaper.

Dee I doubt it, but I take your point.

Stone Their end being your beginning you might say. And a jolly good hour on the telly in the bargain. (*He smiles and then looks at his watch and, making it sound light*) Come along now, Helen. (*He stands*) I'll just ... umm ... (*He indicates "pop in and see her"*)

Dee Fine.

Stone Probably doing her hair or something. Making herself presentable for our famous visitor.

Dee smiles awkwardly

Excuse me ... (*He opens the bedroom door*) Come along now, Helen ...

He exits into the bedroom, closing the door behind him

Dee knocks back her vodka, grimacing at the size of the glass, and then again notices the pile of books. Just as a matter of interest, she gets up and moves to the coffee table, flips through the books to see their titles //

Dee (*wearily, sotto voce*) Oh dear oh dear oh dear ...

Stone enters from the bedroom, turning back to speak into the room

Stone Yes, we've got a drink and we're perfectly happy—aren't we, Miss Redmond?

Dee (*calling dutifully*) Fine.

Stone There we are, you see—no rush, darling, no rush. (*He closes the door*) Just as I thought—(*he flutters his fingers at his head*)—titivating. (*But more seriously*) She has these moods when she can't quite—connect. Can't quite—tie things together. As I say, it's these pills, these pain-killers. (*He sits on the sofa and stares into his glass*)

Dee (*moving to sit next to him*) Does she ... does she know?

Stone (*sighing*) Oh yes. (*After a slight pause*) Six months they think.

Dee And she's—coping.

Stone (*frowning*) People seem to find an inner strength.   //

Dee And you?

Stone (*looking up*) Have you ever known death, Miss Redmond? Someone close?   //

A slight pause

Dee No.

Stone Strange, really. That you should write about it all the time. That your very first play should be concerned with it. With more than death. With murder. (*With a change of tone*) Oh dear oh dear oh dear we're getting morbid—let me get you another drink ...

During the next few speeches, he replenishes her glass, getting ice from the kitchen etc.

(*Brightly*) I suppose you must get people writing to you all the time.

Dee Umm—yes—some.

Stone I hope you didn't feel that I was pressurizing you. When I telephoned.

Dee A little—yes. Until you explained the circumstances.

Stone Actually ... I was surprised your number's in the book.

Dee It's my one grand gesture towards humility.

Stone (*moving to stand near her; confidentially*) To be very honest ... Helen doesn't know I phoned you. She thinks *you* phoned *us*.

Dee Oh. (*She glances instinctively towards the bedroom*)

Stone Yes. When you didn't reply to her letter——

Dee makes to interject, but he continues straight on

—she was quite depressed—which is why I took it upon myself to telephone and explain. How much it would mean to her.

Dee I know this is going to sound like a terrible excuse—but I couldn't find her letter—the covering letter she sent with the script ...

Stone Oh, you brought it back with you, did you? (*He moves across to take up the envelope from the armchair*)

Dee Usually I file everything away very meticulously but for some reason I seem to have made a boob. So it's just as well you telephoned, otherwise ...

Stone And what did you think of it?

Dee (*lying*) It's not bad.

He moves closer to her and indicates that they should both speak quietly

Stone Please—you can be honest with me.

Dee It's not bad—but—it's not really very good. I honestly don't think I could recommend it. I mean I could *try*, but ...

A moment

Stone I'd be grateful if you could give her—well—a little ray of hope. If you could say *something* nice.

Dee Of course I will. (*In an entirely instinctive moment she reaches out to touch the back of his hand comfortingly. But the moment becomes almost instantly awkward and she withdraws the hand and takes up her glass to drink*)

Stone (*as though brightly charging the subject*) Have you managed to sell your flat?

She looks at him

You were trying to sell your flat.

Dee I seem to have told you my entire life story.
Stone Sorry?
Dee When you phoned.
Stone Oh—yes—(*smiling*)—you did seem very chatty, I must say. //

Dee looks at him and then knocks back her drink and instantly he takes up her glass

Dee Thank you—no.
Stone (*moving to the drinks table*) Just a little one—I'm having one.
Dee (*more to herself*) Yes—all right, thanks, why not?
Stone They're not very large glasses anyway, I'm afraid. (*He replenishes her glass, but not his own*)
Dee I don't remember telling you about the flat. I mean, why would I do that?
Stone You thought at first that was why I was phoning. About the flat. You were expecting a call. A potential buyer.
Dee Was I?
Stone You don't remember.
Dee No. (*She manages a smile*) Memory like a sieve.
Stone That's why you have such a meticulous filing system, is it?
Dee (*with a sudden flash of irritation*) No, I haven't sold my flat, thank you.
Stone (*giving her the drink*) Where do you think it mainly goes wrong? The story.
Dee (*indicating the Acting Editions*) She reads a lot of whodunits, does she?
Stone Ah. Too much borrowing of ideas you mean.
Dee We all borrow ideas: it's how you dress them up.
Stone I thought she had rather a good idea with the policeman. Policemen in plays always strike me as so very difficult.
Dee In the main—although I hate to admit it—it's how good your actor is. What *he* brings to the part.
Stone (*moving behind her*) But her idea of making the policeman not the hunter as it were ... but the hunted. I thought that was rather good.
Dee Yes, yes it is. (*She smiles*) And I'll tell her so.
Stone And that business with the telephone. Page seven. Very clever I thought. (*He moves to take up the envelope*)
Dee I'm sorry to say I didn't really understand it.
Stone Oh—well—that was *my* idea actually.
Dee Ooops.
Stone (*with a mounting, almost boyish enthusiasm*) You see ... it seems to me that people are always using the telephone in plays—it always seems to me far too convenient—so I said to her—use the telephone, yes, but try to do it in a way that's different.

Dee smiles brightly, holds up the top Acting Edition

Dee Like—say—*Dial 'M' for Murder*.
Stone (*not to be put down*) Have you ever had your telephone repaired, Miss Redmond?
Dee Once or twice, yes.

Stone Ah! So have we. And I noticed—when the engineer chappie wanted to check the line—there was a particular code number he dialled. You dial one-seven-four or one-seven-five and the last four digits of your own number, replace the receiver, wait—and it rings. Then you know that the line is working. So ... (*He puts the envelope on the arm of the sofa and moves to the telephone*) Let us say for the sake of the plot that you're here and I want you to believe that someone is telephoning me. I make an excuse to ring a number—any number—say ... a cinema. I dial—(*he dials*)—the numbers I've just explained to you. I wait. Tell you the line is engaged or something and replace the receiver. (*He replaces the receiver*) I pretend to move away—(*he moves away*)—and the telephone rings.

The telephone rings. Stone takes up the receiver as though listening

Nine-three-two-nine, hello, yes? (*To Dee*) What I'm actually getting is the dialling tone but you don't know that, you think someone has phoned and I'm making an arrangement, say, arranging a meeting. (*Into the receiver*) You'll be here at eight o'clock.... Good-bye then George ... or Charlie ... or Clive. (*He replaces the receiver*) Try it.

Dee I'll take your word for it.

Stone It's a good idea, isn't it?

Dee Very good, yes.

Stone And it would work.

Dee Would work very well.

Stone Worth borrowing, would you say?

Dee (*smiling*) I'll try not to.

Stone (*with mock-humility*) There are quite a few ideas of mine in that story, actually.

Dee (*lightly*) You're quite sure you didn't write the whole thing?

Stone smiles, pleased. During the following speech, he takes up the envelope casually and puts it on the desk

Stone She tells me her ideas and I try to help her work out the details—I've got that sort of mind, you see. (*He frowns and again attempts a brightness*) Didn't I read somewhere that Agatha Christie got a lot of her ideas from her husband?

Dee Probably. Behind every great woman detective writer there's a little archaeologist. Or something like that.

Stone (*smiling*) For all I know, you get your ideas from *your* husband.

Dee No such luck. There isn't one.

Stone But all those things you write about policemen—I mean, how do you know so much about the procedures—the *attitudes*?

Dee It's called research.

Stone You mean you actually deal with the police.

Dee I have what is known in the trade as a "tame policeman".

Stone Oh I *see* ... you know a policeman——

Dee Yes.

Stone —and he advises you.

Dee Yes.

Stone Ah! Yes, of course. Stupid of me.

A moment. And suddenly Dee is conscious of the time and she looks at her watch

Dee Umm ...

But Stone is off on an enthusiastic trip again

Stone They're really very popular though, aren't they? Detective stories. I was speaking to this chappie at the library—of all the books they keep, the most popular by far are detective stories, whodunits, thrillers. All those little writers tippy-tapping away—it's a veritable cottage industry. We all love a good detective story—we all love a good whodunit, a good murder. I wonder why? I wonder what the fascination is?

Dee gets up and crosses to collect her bag. She takes it back to the sofa

Dee (*lighting a cigarette*) I suppose ... I suppose it's because they're like a crossword puzzle. A crossword puzzle where you know the ending will be supplied even if you get all the clues wrong. Where "good ultimately triumphs over evil" boom-boom. Not like life in other words.

Stone Sorry?

Dee Life. You know, that old thing. Life. With it's anti-climaxes and its—messy endings.

Stone (*"lightly"*) Oh dear.

Dee "Oh dear" what? (*She has tried not to sound sharp but has failed*)

Stone "Messy endings"?

Dee You think I meant me.

Stone Well I ...

Dee Wrong. (*She smiles humourlessly*)

Stone Ah. Well umm ... (*He looks decidedly embarrassed*)

Dee (*still with an edge*) I'm sorry.

Stone I had no right to ... probe. (*He smiles, generous in the knowledge that he has achieved his aim*)

Dee is irritated by his smile, and by his deliberate use of the word "probe", so that her sharp edge continues, making her that fraction more vulnerable ... which again is the continuation of his aim

Where were we? Ah yes ... The population of this country is, what, fifty million? And how many murders—actual murders—are there a year? What, one a week? No, let's be generous—say two, two a week.

Dee Oh yes, let's be generous, let's say three.

Stone Say a hundred and fifty a year then. Most of them a man killing his wife or her lover or his girl-friend or something like that ...

Dee "Domestics."

Stone Sorry?

Dee "Domestic murder." That's what they call it.

Stone Anyway—like in your first play. A—"domestic". So, in reality, just a tiny tiny minority are actually touched by the act of murder. And yet—or maybe because of that—we're all fascinated by it.

Dee Not quite all, surely?

Stone But most wouldn't you say? Look at someone like John Reginald Halliday Christie——

Dee No thanks.

Stone —where they had to change the name of the street because so many people came to stare. Just stare. (*He looks at her intently*) //

Dee (*becoming uneasy and trying to speak lightly*) Now *you*'re staring.

Stone Mmm? Oh, I'm so sorry. (*He smiles*) On something of a hobby-horse. (*He gets up and moves to stand behind the trunk*) Could *you* live in a house where you knew murder had taken place? A particularly brutal murder . . . where a knife had been used, where the blood was everywhere . . . where an innocent soul was hacked to death?

Dee I . . . very much doubt it.

Stone I once lived in a house like that. I'm one of the tiny tiny minority.

Dee (*quietly*) How terrible. (*After a moment*) You mean . . . you lived there afterwards.

Stone Oh, yes, afterwards. Of course. But there was still the knowledge. For all the bright new wallpaper and the bleach-scrubbed floors . . . there was still the knowledge. (*A slight moment*) I couldn't stand it. (*He smiles*) Not surprisingly. Perhaps I should tell you about it one day. You can use me for research. (*Behind her back he glances from the window then turns to her*) You know, I've always wondered what makes a man—or woman—sit down and work out these incredibly complicated plots about murder.

Dee It's called "an eye on the box office". Or putting it another way—art for art's sake, money for Chrissake.

Stone (*moving back to her*) We all have to live.

Dee Indeed we do.

Stone And die.

A moment   //

Dee Shouldn't you see if your wife . . .

Stone I wonder if the real fascination hasn't something to do with envy?

Dee Envy. Of a murderer.

Stone Perhaps not envy. Admiration, sneaking admiration.

Dee Admiration for the man who, say, murders a child. Yes, that seems fair enough.

Stone (*shocked*) No, not that sort of murderer . . .

Dee What sort of murderer did you have in mind? (*She moves away from him, scarcely concealing her irritation*)

Stone I mean the man who plans and executes a murder as a means to his own ends. Be it release . . . or profit . . . or plain and simple hate. In the same way that we admire the thief—not the tuppenny happenny little housebreaker—the thief on the grand scale—The Great Train Robber— the man who plans in one fell swoop to take what the rest of us struggle for throughout a lifetime. Isn't murder, the taking of life, the ultimate theft? A theft of which all of us are capable—given the right set of circumstances? (*He glances from the window*) "There is no crime of which man is not capable." (*He turns from the window, so that he is looking* *directly at her*) And the will to destroy is common enough—how many times do we think—even if we don't say—"I wish you were dead"?

A moment. Dee's irritation has turned to strange unease

Dee Mr Stone—I really am very sorry—but unless your wife ...

Stone (*clapping his hands together with boyish enthusiasm*) Suppose there is no wife? Suppose I've lured you here with a pack of lies, total lies?

Dee (*trying to play the game, but with mounting unease*) Why would you do that?

Stone Because I want to kill you.

Dee (*with a coy "Southern Belle" accent*) But Mister Stone, sir, we've only just met.

Stone Does that matter?

Dee Oh I'd like to think you had a motive.

Stone Is motive really necessary?

Dee Oh, I think so, don't you?

Stone And to have a motive I'd have to know you.

Dee Unless you're working under contract.

Stone You mean someone you *do* know is paying me.

Dee It's that Italian waiter I didn't tip last week. He's a member of the Mafia. I should have known when he didn't help me on with my coat.

Stone It has been known—the hired killer.

Dee Hasn't it just? Although I'm constantly surprised at their incompetence. They invariably seem to miss and hit a dog.

Stone I was thinking of the murder committed without apparent reason.

Dee Oh, there's always a motive, surely?

Stone What if I just wanted to kill someone—anyone—to prove that I could get away with it? That's been known too, hasn't it?

Dee Isn't the motive something to do with the gratification of ego?

Stone A warped ego, you mean.

Dee A nutcase, that's what I mean.

Stone "The balance of the mind being disturbed." Of course, there is a theory that murder can only be committed in a moment of insanity.

Dee It's a theory I'm quite fond of, actually.

Stone On the other hand ... it could be the moment of ultimate sanity. The absolutely justifiable thing to do—given a certain set of circumstances.

Dee I know it's awfully boring but if someone intends knocking me off I really would like it to be because of something I could understand.

Stone How about revenge?

Dee Revenge. Ah!

Stone You accept revenge as a motive for murder?

Dee Oh, I think so.

Stone There was a case in the newspaper only last week. It's quite astonishing how the mind can fester. Especially if it has nothing else to exercise it.

Dee Good old paranoia. My profession swears by it.

Stone A very common condition I understand. Particularly amongst the middle-aged.

Dee (*brightly*) Well—here I am—what's it to be?

Stone The gun?

Dee Too noisy.

Stone The knife then.

Dee Too messy.

Stone And yet quite commonplace. The moment of anger, the weapon conveniently to hand ...

Dee But we're not dealing with anger, are we? Or are we? I can be quite good at making people angry if that's what you want.

Stone (*smiling*) No.

Dee How about straightforward strangulation—although I've always regarded that as rather personal and since we hardly know each other ...

Stone (*holding the smile*) Besides which, you look far too capable.

Dee I'm even tougher than I look. You'd certainly have to—(*she flutters a hand*)—lower the odds.

Stone How about a drink? (*He points*) A few pain-killers, a few sleeping tablets, crushed up and washed down with three vodka and tonics would do it very nicely, I would have thought.

Against her will Dee finds herself looking at her glass. And Stone smiles and takes up a chair cushion

Once you're nice and drowsy ... the cushion goes over the face ... (*He makes a slight movement with the cushion*)

Dee automatically puts up an arm to fend it off. A moment. Does he mean it or doesn't he? But he replaces the cushion and neatly pats it into place

Fairly painless and certainly lacking in complication, wouldn't you say? (*He moves away*) Of course there's always the question of the disposal of the body ... (*He sits on the trunk*) But with the right sort of planning even that can be catered for. (*Suddenly concerned*) I'm very sorry—I didn't frighten you, did I?

Dee The only thing that frightens me, Mr Stone, is trying to do my VAT.

Stone I get rather carried away, I'm afraid ...

Dee I thought I was the one to be carried away. In that thing.

He realizes she means the trunk, looks down at it, sort of laughs, and stands

Stone Yes. (*Behind her back he again glances from the window, this time reacting slightly*)

Dee Course the thing is ... if you *had* decided to knock me off—just to show you could get away with it and nothing personal you understand—I wouldn't have had the chance of telling your wife how promising her story is.

Stone (*laughing*) No. (*Suddenly concerned*) Where is she? Excuse me ... (*He moves quickly towards the bedroom and opens the door*) Helen ...? Helen?

He exits into the bedroom, closing the door behind him

Left alone, Dee takes up her glass and sniffs it. She puts down the glass, stands up and is about to take up her bag

Stone enters suddenly, very concerned and holding a small empty pill bottle. He closes the door behind him, apparently in something of a dither //

Dee What's happened?
Stone Mmm? Sorry? No, it's all right, it's all right ... It's her pills, she ... They might be in the kitchen—I wonder if you'd ...

Dee goes quickly into the kitchen and looks around. As she does so, Stone swiftly takes up the envelope, folds it and puts it into the pocket of his jacket

Dee I can't see them.
Stone Ah yes, briefcase—they're in my briefcase.

Dee comes out of the kitchen

What the hell have I done with my briefcase...? (*He runs his fingers through his hair. As though suddenly remembering*) It's in the car, I must have left it in the car ... Excuse me ... (*He moves towards the lobby, dipping into his trouser pocket*) Keys ... ah yes ... (*He returns to snatch up his jacket from the back of the chair*) I'm so sorry—please—if you could just bear with me ... //

Dee Mr Stone, don't you think it would be better if I——

Stone exits hurriedly, leaving the front door ajar

—go.

Dee stands for a moment, in the wake of the whirlwind. Then she makes up her mind, takes up her cigarettes and her bag and makes to go out, but then, on second thoughts, she moves back to tap gently at the bedroom door. As she does, the bedroom lights up. In the bed, the shape of a body can be seen, someone sleeping, just the dark hair of a woman's head visible above the covers. Dee waits a moment and taps again

Mrs Stone? It's Dee Redmond ... Are you all right? Mrs Stone? (*She tentatively makes to push open the bedroom door*)

At this moment the doorbell rings. Dee starts slightly and turns towards the front door

Hallett pushes open the front door and enters, wearing his hat and coat

For a moment, they stand looking at each other

John ... (*She moves close to him*)
Hallett (*putting his hands gently on her shoulders*) What the hell's this?
Dee (*quietly*) I don't know. (*More firmly*) I don't know, John. (*She puts her arms around him, seeking comfort*) Why are you here?
Hallett I'm supposed to be working. A man called Stone ...
Dee Mr Stone, yes.
Hallett And you?

She looks at him for a moment

Dee His wife. I came to see his wife.

Hallett His wife is dead.

Again she looks at him

~~**Dee** No, she's ... (*She tails off*)~~
~~**Hallett** Dee ...~~
Dee (*pulling away*) What d'you mean "dead", why do you say she's ...
Hallett (*firmly but still gently*) Where is she, Dee?

She looks at him, then towards the bedroom. A moment. Then Hallett moves into the bedroom. Dee stands in the doorway as Hallett looks down at the figure in the bed. He moves to touch the figure gently, then suddenly grasps the hair and lifts it—and the head comes away in his hand. He turns it towards the audience and it can be seen that it is composed of a woman's wig and a balloon, on to which has been stuck an enlarged photograph of a smiling young woman's face, the lips of which have been painted in a shocking red. Dee stifles a scream. And Hallett jerks back the covers to show that the "body" is composed of pillows. Then he quickly drops the "head" and moves to comfort Dee, putting his arms around her

   (*Gently*) It's all right, Dee ... it's all right ...
Dee Why?
Hallett Someone playing silly buggers. (*With a change of tone*) I don't know why: but I'll soon bloody well find out.

Dee moves away from him quickly and snatches up the pill bottle as Hallett stands jiggling coins in his pocket

Dee He said he was going downstairs to get her some more pills. I believed him absolutely. I mean, why shouldn't I? He even showed me the bottle. Look. (*She thrusts the pill bottle into his hand*)

He looks down at the label as Dee moves away uneasily and vaguely indicates the bedroom

   You've no idea who the pretty lady is meant to be, I suppose?

Hallett doesn't seem to hear. He stands frowning slightly at the bottle. Dee makes up her mind suddenly

   (*Firmly*) I want to go, John ... I want to get out of here ...
Hallett Now take it easy ...
Dee I want to *go* ... Whatever it is, I want to get out of here ... (*She makes to move past him to get her bag*)
Hallett (*gently and firmly catching her arm*) Dee ... Look at the label.
Dee I don't want to look at the ...
Hallett Look at the label.

Something in his voice makes her stop. A moment. Then she takes the bottle from him, looks at it, then slowly up at him

   Prescribed for *you*, Dee: they're yours.
She sits slowly on the sofa, staring at the bottle as the Lights fade slowly to a Black-out and—

                    the CURTAIN *falls*

ACT II

The same. A few moments later

The bedroom is now in darkness. Hallett's hat and coat have been thrown over a chair

Dee sits on the sofa, smoking nervously. Hallett is looking into the junk cupboard. He closes the doors, clearly having been unable to find anything of interest. He turns, looks down at the trunk, moves to it and flips at the padlock, then goes to the desk and quickly and methodically looks through the drawers. He leaves the drawers open

Hallett Nothing.

Dee (*with an edge to her voice*) I see.

Hallett No papers, no letters, nothing.

Dee We've all got papers. From the minute we're born we've got papers. It's one of the joys of the Welfare State. (*She looks at him sharply*) So why hasn't *he*? (*She stubs out her cigarette violently*)

Hallett thrusts his hands into his pockets and stands, jingling the coins in his pocket. Irritated by him, she gets out another cigarette

Hallett (*gently*) You don't really need that, do you, Dee?

Dee Don't tell me what to do, thankyousomuch. (*She lights the cigarette*) And if we're on about irritating little habits, stop jangling your bloody money.

A moment. As though to placate her, he lights one of his cigars

Hallett (*slowly, as though working it out*) He got you here ... he got me here ... which means he knows us ... which means he could know *about* us.

Dee (*with a sarcastic edge*) Perhaps your wife also knows about us. Perhaps she's enlisted his services rather than those of a solicitor. (*With her smile*) That's it, wouldn't you say?

Hallett No.

Dee You're that sure, are you, John?

Hallett (*with a slight shrug, clearly placating*) All right—it's possible.

Dee In which case, things being out in the open at last, you might have to consider making an honest woman of me, rather than having your cake and stuffing it as and when you ...

Hallett Stop it, Dee ... for Chrissake stop it.

Dee Oh yes of course, I musn't pressurize you ...

Hallett Is this the time ... *is it?*

Dee Is it ever "the time"? (*She looks at him angrily, but can't hold the look and turns away*)

He remains looking at her. Whatever sympathy he might feel for her edgy state is tinged with irritation, the muscles of his jaw flexing. A moment

Hallett You go, Dee.

She looks at him, not understanding

Come on, I'll walk you to your car. (*He moves to her*)
Dee You mean you're staying.
Hallett It isn't finished.
Dee You think he'll be back.
Hallett I'd lay odds on it.
Dee Oh well, why didn't you say before? I mean, he's such stimulating company—perhaps he'll do that trick with the cushion again—I really enjoyed that.
Hallett He got you here, he got me here. He deliberately arranged for us to be alone together. He's put us in a frame and he wants to make us sweat. (*He indicates the pill bottle*) Why else would he make sure you saw these?

A moment. Then she gets up and moves to him and puts her arms around him

Dee I'm scared, John. I'm really ~~afraid~~ *frightened*

He puts his arms around her and kisses her gently, briefly

Hallett He's playing games with us, Dee. I want to find out why. And to do that, maybe *we*'ll have to play games. Or at least *I* will.

Dee looks at him and is about to say something when the sound of a key in the front door is heard. Hallett gives Dee a little sign implying "Take it easy, it's all right"

Stone enters. He is all expansive bonhomie. A little too expansive to quite conceal the tension he himself feels

Stone Sorry to keep you—you were expecting me, weren't you?
Hallett (*spreading his hands; friendly*) Wouldn't have been the same without you.
Stone Do sit down, Miss Redmond.
Dee No thanks.
Stone As you please. Did you give Mr Hallett a drink? Whisky and water, isn't it?
Hallett Thanks all the same—(*his flat smile*)—I never drink when I'm off duty.
Stone I do enjoy a sense of humour.
Hallett I like bread and butter pudding m'self.
Dee For God's sake ... who are you?
Stone I've told you who I am. (*He looks at the open desk drawers and closes them neatly*) Although it seems you didn't believe me. I thought that might be the case.

Behind his back, Hallett indicates for Dee to sit. She does so, unwillingly. Hallett sits, apparently relaxed, away from her

"When they got there, the cupboard was bare." Cleaned out, in fact. (*He frowns*) Shouldn't you have a search-warrant to do this sort of thing?

Hallett Why don't you phone the nick and find out?

Stone I could—but then I'd rather save Miss Redmond the embarrassment.

Dee Why should I be embarrassed?

Stone (*pseudo-coyly*) Come now, Miss Redmond ... carrying on with a married man? surely even *you* would go slightly pink around the cheeks?

Dee "Carrying on"? What a quaint old-fashioned thing you are, Mr Stone.

Stone (*smiling*) Are you quite sure you wouldn't like a drink?

Dee What do you want?

Stone Under the circumstances, I thought we should have a little talk. (*He perches on the trunk*)

Hallett Okay—so waddaya want to talk about?

Stone Can't you guess?

Hallett Give us a clue, why don't you?

Stone Oh yes, of course, you like clues, don't you? Being "a detective". (*He smiles*) I would have thought I'd given you enough. If not to put you one step ahead, at least to set you on an equal footing. What I will say is that it's something we're all very much concerned with—each in our own way.

Dee Which is *what*?

Stone Which is ... the business of murder. (*He stands*) Do let me get you a drink—I know you'll need one. (*He smiles amiably and moves into the kitchen*)

Dee turns anxiously to Hallett and he makes a little gesture, reminding her to leave it to him, to stay calm

During the next few speeches, Stone takes a bowl of ice from the fridge, then moves to the drinks table to prepare three drinks—vodka and tonic, neat whisky and sherry, each measured in his irritatingly precise way

Hallett (*taking up his cigar and relighting it*) The business of murder.

Stone "Business" being the operative word. That is—"business" in the sense of "habitual occupation, profession, trade"—applying to you—(*he indicates them both*)—and "business" in the sense of "the thing that concerns one, the thing that one may meddle with"—applying to me.

Dee suddenly gives a little laugh, shaking her head

Dee He's out of his mind ... He's out of his mind and we're sitting here *listening* to him.

Stone The reason you're still sitting here is not because you suspect that I might be mad but because of a greater suspicion that I might be only too sane.

Dee No wife, no son.

Stone I'm afraid not.

Dee Figments of your—pardon me—warped imagination.

Stone You invent characters, Miss Redmond—would you describe your imagination as warped? *The Daily Telegraph* describes it as "fertile". I think that's much better, don't you? But yes, you're absolutely right, I invented a particular son, a particular wife, in order to arouse your interest.

Dee To get us here.

Stone To get you here. Yes.

Dee So that we could have our little "talk".

Stone Not—quite. There were other things that needed to be done. That necessitated your participation as it were. But more or less. Yes.

Stone takes the vodka and tonic to Dee and holds it out to her. After a moment, she takes it, aware of her weakness in doing so. She tosses back a mouthful in defiance of that weakness. Stone hands the whisky to Hallett

Hallett Things that needed to be done. Like putting your little chum to bed.

Stone (*smiling*) Just my little joke, I'm afraid.

Hallett Yeah, we had quite a laugh.

They smile "amiably" at each other then Stone takes up his drink

Hallett I take it the name Stone is something else assumed for our benefit.

Stone Not entirely for your benefit, I'm afraid, although it does have a proverbial relevance you might say.

Hallett The proverbial "stone".

Stone I should point out that the relevance struck me only as an after-thought.

Hallett The proverbial stone ... gathers no moss.

Stone It also kills two birds. Or so they say. Given the right circumstances. (*He toasts them with his sherry*) Cheers.

Dee gets up and moves away angrily, nervously. She takes up the bottle of pills and turns to face Stone

Dee Where did these come from?

Stone From where you left them.

Dee (*to Hallett; firmly*) They were in my bathroom, in my flat.

Stone That's right.

Dee You've never been to my flat.

Stone Oh, but I have. You invited me there. In a manner of speaking.

A moment

Dee (*trying to remain calm*) You're saying you've been to my flat.

Stone Yes.

Dee And that I invited you there.

Stone As I say ...

Dee Liar.

Stone All it needs ... is thinking about.

Dee looks at him, sits down and lights a cigarette with a hand that shakes

You're not still nervous, Miss Redmond?

She looks at him hatefully

Hallett Oh come on, Dee, say you're nervous, don't spoil the man's fun, he's enjoying himself.

Dee Listen to you! You're enjoying it as much as he is.

Stone Oh, but Mr Hallett understands, you see. That's how policemen operate, isn't it, Mr Hallett? First, prime the subject. Lower his resistance, weaken his morale and then—when he's tired, afraid, off-guard—in for the kill. But *you* know that, Miss Redmond, you've written the scene often enough. The good policeman tries all manner of tricks—just as long as the end justifies the means. Which it always does—on television at least. There is, after all, the image to protect. (*He smiles*) No need to be nervous, surely—not when you have a very capable Superintendent of Police sitting not ten feet away and liable to flick ash all over my carpet.

He takes up the ashtray and holds it out to Hallett who deliberately flicks ash on to the carpet but then suddenly grips Stone's wrist

Hallett We're here. Now say what you want.

Stone Are you arresting me, Superintendent?

Hallett Now why should I do that?

Stone Then take your hand off me.

A moment

Hallett Enjoy it while you can, Mr Stone. (*After a moment, he releases his grip, knocks back his drink and gets up to pour himself another*)

Dee (*as though to herself*) It's something we've done.

Stone Sorry?

Dee That's why we're here. Because of something we've done. (*She looks at Stone*) Isn't it?

Stone You see, I knew if I could persuade you to stay it would stimulate your—fertile imagination.

Dee For God's sake stop it!

Stone Ninteen seventy-five, September nineteen seventy-five.

Hallett That's supposed to mean something is it?

Stone More to me than it does to you, obviously.

Hallett Dee?

Dee (*sighing*) September nineteen seventy-five. I was working on a news-paper.

Stone Which newspaper?

Dee The *Echo*, the *North London Echo*.

Stone The Stanmore edition. Stanmore being where Mr Hallett was stationed. Detective *Inspector* Hallett as he was then.

Dee We didn't know each other.

Stone No, that came later.

Dee Is there anything about us you don't know?

Stone (*smiling*) Not everything. But then, who knows everything about anybody?

Dee Oh, come on—don't be modest—I'll bet you even know my National Insurance number.

Stone ZB one-three eight-four five-nine C. Of course, you won't remember it—perhaps you'd like me to write it down so that you can ...
Dee You've made your point, thank you.

A moment

Hallett September seventy-five.
Stone September the fourteenth to be precise.
Hallett I'm very bad on dates—why don't I phone the nick and get 'em to send round my diary?
Stone By all means. (*He indicates the telephone*)

Hallett sits down

No? Then let me refresh your memory. You were on night duty. "Late turn", I think you call it. At approximately eleven-fifteen you were called to number twenty-three Haversham Crescent. You can remember *that*, surely Mr Hallett?
Dee (*suddenly aware*) John ...
Hallett I can remember.
Stone You were called to the house by a neighbour—a Mrs Darbon. She had heard noises, went to the house, found the door open and as a result of what she saw, telephoned the police station. The "nick". (*After a slight pause*) The woman was lying in the hallway. She had been stabbed eleven times with what tests would later show to be a double-sided knife. The boy was at the top of the stairs. He had been stabbed nine times—with the same knife—and had also been severely beaten about the head and face with an instrument that was never determined. The fingers of both his hands had been almost severed. It would seem that he had put up something of a fight. He was nine years old. Would have been nine years old, the following month. (*A slight smile*) And so you set about your business, Mr Hallett. As it turned out, it wasn't so very difficult because at seven o'clock the following morning you apprehended me on a charge of murder.

A moment

Dee (*quietly*) Metcalfe. David Charles Metcalfe.
Stone Of course, I wear these things now—(*indicating his glasses*)—and I've lost far too much weight and I, I'm told, aged quite considerably. But then, even if I hadn't it isn't the most memorable of faces, is it? How would you describe it if I were a character in one of your plays, Miss Redmond? Ordinary? Average? Nondescript? The sort of face you'd see a thousand times in a thousand places—see, but not look at. Not like you're looking at me now.

A moment

Nothing to say?
Hallett What do you want us to say?
Stone Yes, I wondered how you'd react. I remember reading once how

Albert Pierrepoint, the executioner, was serving behind the bar of his pub one night—somewhere in Liverpool, I think it was—when a man who had been drinking there for about half an hour—a stranger, a Pole, I believe—said to him, "You don't know me, do you?" And Pierrepoint said "No", and the man said "Ten years ago today you were measuring me with a view to putting a rope around my neck." It turned out that the man was due to be hanged but was granted a last-minute reprieve. "Well I never," said Mr Pierrepoint and bought him a drink. Then the man bought him one and they shook hands and never saw each other again.

Hallett So you've changed. People do.

Stone You haven't changed, Mr Hallett. You're exactly as I remember. Arrogant ... self-opinionated ... very, very sure of yourself. (*He turns and smiles at Dee*) Of course, we've never met, Miss Redmond, not in the flesh as it were, so whether or not ...

Dee Then why am I here? What do you want from me?

Stone Ah. You mean you can understand what I want from Mr Hallett ...

Dee I didn't say that. I don't know what you want from either of us.

Stone Are you sure, Miss Redmond? Not just the tiniest little glimmer?

Hallett Perhaps he wants me to buy *him* a drink.

Stone You'll notice I said "apprehended" and not "arrested" on a charge of murder. Although he did try, my goodness me how he tried.

Hallett I had good reason.

Stone Just doing your job, yes of course you were.

Dee Everything was against you—you must see that now, even if you ... (*She tails off*)

Stone Even if I didn't see it then. Circumstances, Miss Redmond—that's all there was against me—circumstances.

Dee It's a word you're very fond of.

Stone It's a word the police are very fond of ... circumstances ... circumstantial evidence ... "establishing the doubtful main fact by inference from known facts otherwise hard to explain". And the doubtful main fact that you tried so rigorously to prove in this case was that I had murdered my own wife and child, that I had gone to that house ...

Hallett Three questions in my game—where, when and why. We knew where, we knew when, what we had to find out was why—and the why pointed straight at *you*.

Stone (*to Dee; smiling*) Motive, there always has to be a motive.

Hallett You were divorced—we found that out in about ten minutes flat—just over a year, since which time there'd been nothing but trouble, nothing but aggravation over the kid ...

Stone Aggravation? You think it's right that she should have lied, made excuses, spread all manner of filth about me being a bad influence on my own *son*?

Hallett It's what I know that matters in my job, not what I think. And what I knew—what I found out because it's my job to find out—was that earlier that same day she'd been to court taking out an order against the husband—who turned out to be *you*—restraining him from seeing the kid ... What I *knew* was that she'd told at least two people that she was worried about your carryings-on ... worried about your "obsessive" behaviour ...

Stone He was my son!

A moment

Dee I think ... I *know* ... why I'm here.

Stone (*calm again*) I think you've known since you discovered my real name.

A slight pause

Dee Yes.

Stone Or, at least, been made aware of our—peculiar relationship.

Dee The man accused of murder ... the investigating officer ...

Stone And the young lady who wrote her very first television play about the events of that night ... because it fascinated her and because it made—what was it?—a jolly good story.

A slight pause

Dee (*awkwardly*) I—I simply wanted to show how what happened that night was possible. I ...

Stone Oh, but I do understand, believe me. After all, it did happen—not quite in the way you portrayed it, but it did happen—and anything that serves to broaden the knowledge and therefore the understanding, the compassion even, of fourteen million viewers must be justified, mustn't it?

Dee I *thought* ... I *hoped* ... (*She tails off*)

Stone You hoped what, Miss Redmond?

Dee (*shaking her head; quietly*) It doesn't matter.

Stone Ah. It doesn't matter.

Dee I didn't mean it like that.

Stone No, of course you didn't. (*To Hallett*) You're very quiet, Mr Hallett.

Hallett Not often. (*He moves to pour himself a drink*)

Stone Not jumping to the lady's defence?

Hallett Does she need defending?

Stone Now where were we? Ah yes—my obsessive behaviour. The scene very early on between you and your sergeant was rather good on that, I thought. Not that it was you and your sergeant, just two actors behaving remarkably like you and your sergeant—well, up to a point. How is he by the way? Still in the job? He struck me as rather uncomfortable, rather—embarrassed by your methods. Or was that all part of your act, your real-life act? The Barlow and Watt you might say. There I go again—it's so difficult to get away from the dreaded box nowadays, isn't it?

Hallett What else do you do besides watch television?

Stone I do watch a great deal, I must admit. Living alone as I do.

Hallett Join a bingo club.

Stone Bingo. Yes. Always worth a cheap laugh. Unless you're looking for somewhere to belong. To be a part of something. To be—accepted. (*With a change of tone*) Yes. The scene between you and your sergeant. Very good, I thought. Now what was it you said? Sorry, the actor said ...

Hallett *I* said. (*A moment*) "Think about it." That's what I said. "Here's a man, divorced, besotted with his kid, living in a sordid little room, on his own, all the time in the world to wind himself up. He goes to the house, demands to see the kid, she tells him about the court order, tries to shut the door in his face . . . he loses his temper, goes bananas . . . 'If I can't have my kid no-one's having him sort of thing' . . . Flips his lid right off, bingo, kills the pair of 'em. God almighty I can almost *see* it happening." (*After a slight pause*) That's what I said, that's how I saw it happening. It wouldn't have been the first time.

Stone No. (*After a slight pause*) No. (*After a moment*) You came to my lodgings, I wasn't there. Piece number one in the circumstantial jigsaw.

Hallett You came back at seven in the morning, you couldn't say where you'd been, you——

Stone I tried. It's not easy to think positively when you've just been informed that your wife and child have been butchered to death.

Hallett I asked where you'd been, you said you'd been out walking. All night you'd been walking but when I ask where, you don't know . . .

Stone That evening I telephoned her, asked to speak to my son and it was then that she told me what she'd done, told me about the court order. If you could have heard her voice. The utter, utter satisfaction. I went out and I walked. In a complete blank. The more I walked the more blank I became. All of which I told you and all of which you refused to believe. Twenty-four hours you kept me in that room. They were dead and I was being accused of killing them, of killing the one thing——

Hallett It had to be done.

Stone Yes.

Hallett No pleasure to me.

Stone Oh, but your *face*, Mr Hallett. Not to mention your fist in my kidneys on one occasion.

Dee (*looking at Hallett*) That isn't true.

Stone No, of course it isn't true. It didn't happen in your play so it can't be true. Can't have an officer of the law losing his temper because he can't get what he wants and punching a man who's defenceless, can we? Punch and Judo? Not good for the image, not good for the image *at all*. Incidentally, we *were* alone at the time. I had just been sick on the floor and the more squeamish sergeant had been despatched for a cup of tea with no sugar. Although on second thoughts perhaps it was my lack of good manners that prompted such a swingeing reprimand.

Dee (*to Hallett*) It isn't true, say it isn't true.

Hallett says nothing—an answer in itself

Stone It was, Miss Redmond, a nightmare. A twenty-four-hour nightmare. Without even the dubious moral value of the end justifying the means.

Hallett You were released.

Stone Oh yes.

Hallett No charges brought.

Stone Not on paper. But to your mind . . .

Hallett To my mind you got away with it.

A moment

Stone And you, Miss Redmond?

Dee looks at him, then looks away, shaking her head slightly

Oh, you believe it too, surely? After all, look at your play. The man is released. We are led to believe that, for all the hard but fair probing of our wonderful police force, the man has shown himself to be innocent, the victim of circumstance. All our sympathies are with him. The horror of his situation. The nightmare. He tries to resume a normal life and then, quite suddenly, he walks out into the night and throws himself under a train and in that moment we come to realize that he was, after all, quite guilty.

Dee It was a play, a fiction ...

Stone A jolly good hour on the telly—with a nice dramatic ending—we must always have a good ending, mustn't we? Far too many complaints about these plays that just——

Dee All right! I thought you *were* guilty, I thought you *had* got away with it. At least ... at least until they arrested that boy.

Stone Yes, what a pity that didn't come two years earlier—you could have had an even bigger sting in your fictional tail. Three old ladies are stabbed to death in their homes—three murders over a period of a year or so and with no apparent motive. The police finally arrest a young man—a psychopath who murders, it would seem, simply for the pleasure. He's tried, found guilty and sent to Broadmoor. And after the trial, the police disclose that at the time my wife and son were murdered, this young man was living in the area, living in a room not two hundred yards away. Coincidence? Possibly. But then their murderer had not been found and the possibility was certainly worth considering. But not by Mr Hallett who informed the press that, as far as he was concerned, the file was still open. And, by inference, the finger was pointed once again at me.

Hallett If you didn't do it, why should it worry you?

Stone Come now—even you aren't that insensitive.

Dee It was his family, for God's sake.

Stone (*smiling*) Thank you.

Hallett So what does he want, an apology?

Dee (*to Stone*) I don't know *what* you want.

Hallett (*sarcastically*) Maybe it's a confession—maybe he wants us to hear a confession.

Stone Of a sort.

Hallett All right, let's hear it.

Stone When I'm ready.

Hallett What if I'm not prepared to wait?

Stone Then you must go. And face the consequences.

Dee What do you *want* from us?

Stone Bear with me, please.

Dee Or face the consequences.

Stone *And* face the consequences.

Dee Of what?

Stone Of what you did to me.

Dee (*trying to maintain calm*) Tell me ... just tell me ... what the hell am I supposed to have done to you?

Stone You made capital out of my despair. I think you owe me a little something in return.

Dee looks at Hallett who gives a little shrug and moves to pour himself another drink as Dee gives a nervous laugh

Dee I came into this house ... with nothing but good intentions ... an hour later ... this. It's like a ...

Stone A nightmare. Yes. Do help yourself, Mr Hallett—perhaps Miss ...?

Hallett Miss Redmond doesn't want a drink, thanks.

Dee Don't tell me what I can or can't do, I'm not your ... (*looking defiantly at Stone*) ... wife.

A moment, which Stone quietly relishes. And then Hallett moves to take Dee's glass and refill it

Stone I walked out of that police station a free man. Of course, everyone was very sympathetic ... *of course* they didn't believe I was guilty ... It was inconceivable that I could kill my own wife and child ... If there's anything we can do—*please.*" But I didn't ask and very soon they stopped offering. Suddenly I was unclean. Start again ... new name, new job, new home. All these things I could change. But what could never change ... is the inside of my head. The knowledge of what had happened that night. I had a breakdown. Treatment. Another lost job, another change of adress. Finally ... this place.

A slight pause

Hallett All of which ... we're responsible for, are we?

A moment. And Stone continues as though he hasn't heard

Stone Eighteen months ... eighteen months after that night ... I was sitting in my room, watching television—yes, watching television, Mr Hallett—and ... there was your play, Miss Redmond. *The Burden of Guilt.* Such a clever title, I thought. And the next day the newspapers were saluting you. Applauding a "bright new talent". Two plays later and a double-spread in the Sunday supplement—even photographs of "the writer at work". Your foot was well and truly on the ladder: how very exciting it must have been.

Hallett Meanwhile, you were falling to pieces. Gimmee a handerkerchief, will you, Dee, I'm gonna cry.

Stone More than cry, Mr Hallett. More than cry.

Hallett Waddaya want me to do? Close the file? Make a public announcement?

Dee (*quietly insistent*) No-one believes you're guilty.

Stone No-one *says* they believe I'm guilty. Apart from Mr Hallett that is— and even then, only by inference.

A slight pause

Hallett Okay, sunshine, you've had your fun—now why don't we go home so you can get back to the telly?

Stone Because I haven't finished with you.

Dee With us? You haven't finished *with* us?

Stone I'd just lost my job. My third job. I went to a pub, to have a drink, to try and work things out. And there you were, Mr Hallett. With some of your—colleagues. From what I overheard, you had just been promoted and this was by way of a celebration. I looked you in the face ... and you didn't even recognize me. You gave me twenty-four hours of hell and you didn't even recognize me. In that moment ... I came to hate you.

Hallett (*raising his eyes to heaven*) Oh dear oh dear oh der.

Stone When you left, I followed you. I didn't know why, I just followed you. You met Miss Redmond. I recognized you from your photographs. From then on ... I followed you all the time. The married policeman and his—bit on the side. The lady writer—and her tame policeman.

Hallett "Tame policeman"? Nice.

Dee My expression, not his.

Hallett (*amused*) That's what you call me, is it, your tame policeman?

Dee I told him I had an advisor—yes—"tame policeman" ... (*Angrily, to Stone*) Yes, you're right, that's how we met—when I started writing the play I needed some inside information, I wanted to make it "real"— someone suggested I should ask John—he'd know more about it than anyone—so we met, talked ...

Stone And kept on meeting. The one thing having led to the other. (*He smiles*)

Dee You don't plan these things. They just ...

Stone Just happen. Oh, indeed they do—although I must admit to being somewhat surprised that a woman of your obvious attraction and intelligence has never found a husband of her own. Too busy furthering your career perhaps?

Dee looks at him angrily

Borrowing someone else's husband always strikes me as so very futile.

Dee (*flatly*) Does it.

Stone More often than not they go back home to Mama: if indeed they ever leave her. But *you* know that, surely, Miss Redmond.

Dee (*attempting sarcasm*) Indeed I do, Mr Stone. It's just that every now and again a working girl gets tired of her typewriter and needs something else to play with. (*She "smiles"*) The typewriter's on hire, too, as it happens.

Hallett Don't excite him, Dee: I shouldn't think he's dipped his wick for years.

Dee (*rounding on him*) That wasn't very clever, was it.

Hallett gives a sardonic little shake of the head that she should attack him for what she herself had done a moment before, and she is aware of it

(*Softly*) Either of us.

Hallett (*to Stone*) Is that your game, is it? Blackmail? Tell the missus? Or . . . or what?

A moment. Stone looks at Hallett with contempt

Stone I was surprised at how much it's possible to know about people—to find out about people—simply by watching them. I began to build up quite a little dossier . . . times, places, dates . . . *The Red Lion* in Putney seems to be a favourite. (*He smiles*) Research, Miss Redmond.

Dee Research for *what?*

Stone I must admit that at the time I wasn't sure. All I knew was that the more I saw of you, the more I knew of you, the more I wanted to pay you back. You were so very pleased with yourselves. Then, one day, I saw the "For Sale" notice go up outside your flat. And everything fell into place. I knew then what I wanted to do—and how I could do it. (*He smiles and sits down*) It's a very charming little flat, Miss Redmond. I really am surprised you haven't managed to sell it. I particularly like the mirrored cupboards in the bedroom.

Dee (*suddenly realizing*) You went to the agent, didn't you?

Stone Ah!

Dee That's what you did . . . you went to the agent, said you were interested, he showed you round—that time I was away, he showed you round.

Stone I said—all it needed was thinking about.

Dee My God. (*She gets up and moves away*)

Stone They're always so very busy, estate agents. So full of their own importance, all those shiny young men justifying their existence—over-fed parasites in Alfa-Romeos. It wasn't difficult to persuade the particular gentleman concerned to let me go on ahead with the key. And on the way . . . to have a copy made.

Dee (*moving back to him*) Are you saying you've been in and out of my flat . . .

Stone Whenever I chose. Yes. And whenever you weren't there, of course. I always checked first.

Dee (*impotently*) I don't believe it.

Hallett You would have been seen.

Stone Oh, I was very careful. Except on the occasions when I wanted to be seen. Then I didn't mind who saw me.

Dee I don't give a damn whether he was seen or not. Didn't you hear what he said? He's been walking in and out of my flat . . .

Stone (*standing*) Does that make me a burglar or a housebreaker? I'm never sure which is which—and anyway, you'd have to prove it, wouldn't you?

Hallett How about *you* proving it?

Stone I give you my word—as a murder suspect and a gentleman.

Dee (*snatching up the pill bottle*) These—that's how he got *these*—that's why he gave them to me, to show just how bloody (*To Stone*) That's how you knew about my car being in for service—you looked in my diary—you went to my desk and you looked in my diary.

Stone gives an open-handed gesture of assent

Stone That's how I found out about a great many things. I must say you do seem to have rather a collection of pills ... pills for all manner of things ... going to sleep, staying awake, calming the nerves ... I suppose it's all down to your artistic temperament. Oh, by the way, I shan't be needing the key anymore—perhaps you'd like it as a spare—it's under the vase there—(*he smiles*)—safekeeping.

A moment. Then Hallett moves to the bookshelves, lifts up the vase, and turns, holding the key. A moment

I did of course remove my fingerprints.

A moment. Then Hallett moves to stand menacingly over Stone

Hallett (*quietly*) On your feet.
Stone Why? So that you can knock me down again?
Hallett On—your—feet.

Suddenly he reaches down and hoists Stone to his feet by his lapels

Dee (*crying out instinctively*) No!

But Hallett is already roughly turning Stone and gripping him by one arm behind his back, pushing him against the wall

Hallett Hands against the wall, legs apart.

Hallett roughly pushes him into position as Dee puts hands to her head, trying to blot out what is happening

Let's see what else you've got ...
Stone Nothing of interest, I can assure you.

Hallett begins to frisk Stone expertly. He takes loose change, keys and a handkerchief from his jacket pockets and tosses them down, takes a wallet from his inside pocket and tosses it to Dee

Just like old times.
Hallett Yeah.
Stone You found nothing then, you'll find nothing now.
Hallett (*to Dee, of the wallet*) Look through this.
Stone Such an ungainly position I always think—and wide-open to misinterpretation. If someone were to walk in and find us like this, Mr Hallett, they might very well assume we were engaged.

Dee makes a half-hearted search of the wallet

Dee (*hopelessly*) What are we supposed to be looking for, tell me what we're looking for.
Stone He doesn't really expect to *find* anything—the real object of this humiliating little exercise is to adjust the balance of power, isn't that right, Mr Hallett?

Hallett moves away, takes the wallet

Dee Just a few cards, driving licence, nothing he hasn't already said.

Hallett looks through the contents anyway

Stone You don't mind if I move? Thank you. (*He straightens up and collects the loose change, keys and handkerchief and pockets them*) I do hope my driving licence is in order. After all this I should hate to be arrested on a mere technicality.
Hallett (*suddenly, brightly*) There y'go, sunshine ...

He tosses the wallett to Stone, who catches it and pockets it. Hallett moves amiably towards Stone, so that they are finally face to face as he speaks

Hallett Sorry about all that ...
Stone My pleasure.
Hallett You do understand ...
Stone Force of habit.
Hallett Getting us here with a load of old moody, well, that's one thing— poking about in someone's private property and doing gawd knows what—well, that's something else, that's something quite naughty.

Suddenly, and still with a smile on his face, he rams a fist into Stone's stomach which sends him crashing back, breathless, into the sofa

Dee Leave him!

Hallett bends to seize Stone's lapels again, pulling him forward in the chair so that their faces are close

Hallett (*quietly*) What have you done?

Stone is breathless, but triumphant in this moment

Stone What I've done ... Mr Hallett ... is what you say I've done ...
Hallett *Tell me ...*
Dee (*putting her hands to her face*) Leave him alone, for God's sake leave him alone!

A moment. And then Hallett releases his grip and Stone falls back into the chair. Hallett moves away, disgusted. Stone straightens his clothing

Stone Murder. That's what I've done, Mr Hallett. Murder.

A moment

Dee (*softly*) He's mad ... I know it, he's mad.
Stone Planned, plotted and executed. In perfect sanity. Murder, bloody murder.

A moment

Hallett (*mockingly*) Anyone I know?
Stone Not as well as you think you know her. Your wife, Mr Hallett, I've murdered your wife.

A slight moment

Hallett I'm supposed to believe that, am I?

Stone If you don't believe it now, you'll believe it soon enough.
Dee He means it, John, I know he means it.
Hallett (*with a sudden flash of irritation*) Just . . . just leave it to me, will you?
(*To Stone*) You—er—you wouldn't like to say when?
Stone About an hour and a half ago. Although time of death can't be
determined all that accurately, can it. They'll narrow it down to the past
three hours or so. Can you totally account for your movements during
that time?
Hallett I won't have to.
Stone (*smiling*) We'll see.

A slight moment

Hallett So you've killed my wife.
Stone Yes.
Hallett What did you do—bore her to death?
Stone I used what I was supposed to have used before. A knife.
Hallett Course you did. ~~You wouldn't~~ like to say why?
Stone Surely you've worked it out by now? No? Ah—well—let me ex-
plain—as simply as I can, you'll appreciate that, I know you will. I have
murdered your good lady and arranged things very carefully so that the
finger points at *you*—that was your expression, wasn't it? The finger
points at you—both of you.

A slight pause

Hallett Nice.
Stone Thank you.
Hallett Always appreciate a good fit-up.
Dee Go there, John—please.
Hallett (*irritably*) Go *where*?
Dee *Her*, for God's sake, *her*.
Hallett (*to Stone, with his smile*) You'd like that, wouldn't you, squire?
You'd like to set me running.
Stone Might I make a suggestion?
Hallett *Please*.
Stone Telephone her. She wasn't going out tonight, was she? Not to your
knowledge anyway.
Hallett Telephone someone you're supposed to have murdered. Why didn't
I think of that? (*To Dee*) *Listen* to him.
Stone You'll find the number engaged. When I called on her this evening I
took the liberty of taking the telephone off the hook. Without her know-
ing, of course. I thought it might convince you that I'd been there. My seal
of arrival as it were. (*Still in some pain and close to vomiting, he moves
towards the lobby*)

Stone exits quickly R *to the bathroom*

Dee (*moving to Hallett; quietly*) He means it, I know he does.
Hallett (*with an edge*) Too much imagination, that's your trouble.
Dee Don't be so bloody . . .

Hallett So bloody *what?* (*He points after Stone derisively*) *Him?*

There is a moment of supressed anger between them. But he makes an effort at conciliation and puts his hands on her arms

(*Making it sound light*) Hey, listen—the last thing we should be doing is . . .
Dee (*pulling away from him*) I want you to phone her.

Hallett looks at her angrily, then with the over-obvious air of a man placating, moves to the telephone and dials

Hallett All right, OK, happy? (*He finishes dialling and puts the receiver to his ear. He listens, and can't stop himself frowning slightly, then makes to replace the receiver*)

Dee moves quickly towards him, takes the receiver and listens

Stone enters, dabbing his face with his handkerchief and putting on his glasses

Hallett takes the receiver from Dee and presses down the rest, then begins to dial again. Dee turns away, and sees Stone regarding them

Stone Yes, try again by all means. Try as often as you like. Or ring the operator, why don't you?
Hallett Come on, Dee, I've had enough of him . . . (*He replaces the reciever and moves to take up his coat and hat*) Dee . . .
Stone Yes, do hurry home. It'll be the first time you've hurried home for years, I would imagine . . . Not that you'll find her there—you don't think I'd do it there, do you? Good Lord no, that wouldn't suit my purpose one iota. If you hurry anywhere I should hurry to Miss Redmond's. Meanwhile I'll telephone your colleagues and have them meet you there—I know there'll be a great many questions they'll want to ask you.

A moment

Hallett (*quietly*) Waddaya mean—Miss Redmond's?
Stone What better way of implicating her?
Dee Why would she go to my flat?
Stone Because I arranged to meet her there.
Hallett She would have said.
Stone No.
Dee Why would she know *you?*
Stone I telephoned her. A month ago. I told her that I was your husband. How distressed I was. How I didn't know which way to turn. How I thought she ought to know. About your—goings-on.
Hallett She would have *said.*
Stone She hated you as much as I do. You don't imagine you're the first, do you—*Dee?* Jack the Lad, home to the missus as and when he feels like it, not even the excuse anymore of how much work there is on his plate . . . you think she didn't *know?* She hated you. When I told her your little bit of stuff was having a baby—not true, of course, icing on the cake—it was all she needed. She couldn't wait to come round and examine your little

love-nest. Jack the Lad. Jack Who Knows Everything. Well, you know *nothing*, Superintendent Hallett-sir—*nothing*.

A moment

Hallett If you've touched her, if you've laid so much as a finger on her, I'll ...

Stone You'll what—kill me? I thought it was only madmen who killed?

A moment. Hallett sits, as though unsure for the first time

Dee If we're capable of saying it ... If we're capable of thinking it ...

Hallett Words.

Dee Not with him.

Hallett Not even someone as sick as him.

Stone Six years ago ...

Hallett There was a reason.

Dee He wants to make us suffer. As he suffered, in exactly the same circumstances—that's it, isn't it?

Stone Bravo.

Hallett Bullshit.

Dee *No.* He wants to—punish us——

Hallett For Chrissake ...

Dee —and to do that, he had to murder. To murder a wife as his wife ...

Hallett Save it for your typewriter.

Dee That's what it's all about, can't you *see*? Can't you understand what he's trying to do? What he's done?

Hallett You need a drink.

Dee That isn't the answer.

Hallett I thought it *was* with you. (*He tosses down his hat and coat over the sofa, takes up Dee's glass and moves to the drinks table*)

Stone I can see he needs some persuading. I shall have to open my little box of tricks. (*He stands behind the trunk and takes out one of his keys, holding it up in the manner of a magician performing a trick. He opens the padlock*)

Dee looks fearfully at Hallett as Stone raises the lid somewhat theatrically and considers the contents

What shall we have? An arm? A leg? A nice piece of fillet? (*He quickly takes a plastic-wrapped tube-shaped parcel from the trunk and makes the gesture of throwing it towards Dee*)

Dee screams, covering herself with her arms

Hallett What the hell! ⹁ ⹁ ⹁ ⹁ ⹁

Dee moves quickly across to Hallett who embraces her

Stone Very poor taste, I do beg your pardon. You have a towel in your bathroom, Miss Redmond. Stolen—or should I say acquired—from the *Hotel La Tremoille* in Paris. I'm afraid I made rather a mess of it. (*Holding the parcel by two corners, he lets it unroll, to reveal a white towel with the* *hotel name embroidered in blue and heavily stained with blood. He slowly lets it fall into the trunk)*

Dee sits on the sofa. Hallett gives her a drink, which she holds in shaking hands

I could, of course, have cut myself shaving.

Hallett You said—a knife.

Stone Yes.

Hallett A knife I haven't touched.

Stone Where did you buy your carving knife, Miss Redmond?

Dee I don't know, I don't know.

Stone Of course you do, it came from Heal's—so often we pay for the name nowadays, don't we?

Hallett I've never even *seen* her knife.

Stone No, but you've seen an identical one. Mine. Bought especially for the purpose. I dropped it—when you first came here—you remember. (*He points to where he dropped the knife*) You were kind enough to pick it up for me. That knife, with your fingerprints and smeared with your wife's blood—has already been disposed of—with one or two other things—on Wimbledon Common. At about the place we met today—you remember we went in your car and got stuck up a lane as a result of my incompetent directions. The mud on your car will show that you were in the area. You could always run it through a car-wash, but it's a question of time, isn't it?

A moment

Your knife, Miss Redmond ... the actual murder weapon and similar in every detail ... is here. (*He takes the plastic bag containing the knife from the trunk and moves to the coffee table. He lets the plastic unroll and the knife drops out on to the table. He returns to the trunk, drops the plastic into it and closes it*) I did hope to perform the task quickly and with the minimum of pain but unfortunately she—er—she realized and put up something of a struggle. In doing so, she tore a button from her assailant's coat. Raincoat. Together with some thread. If you look under your lapel, Mr Hallett, you'll see what I mean.

A moment. Then Hallett takes his coat, turns back the lapels ... to find the top button missing, torn away

When they find the button—and they will—there'll be very little problem in matching it, wouldn't you say?

A moment

You seem stunned, Mr Hallett. I know the feeling. Difficult to know what to say, isn't it, when you've just been informed that your wife has been murdered. However you behave, cause for suspicion. The grief comes later. At least it did with me.

Hallett Why would I kill my wife?

Dee Isn't that what *he* said? Isn't that exactly what *he* said?

Stone Put yourself in the place of the investigating officers. Officer A to Officer B ... "Think about it ... here's a woman, childless, wickedly

informed that her her husband is having an affair with a younger woman
who's pregnant by him ... She goes to their little love-nest, confronts him,
they argue, he loses his temper, something he's not exactly unknown for,
takes up the knife and in this moment of rage ... bingo, he kills her. I can
almost *see* it happening. It wouldn't be the first time." Unquote.

Hallett Except that it's a pack of lies.

Stone They'll need a great deal of convincing. Policeman are so very scepti-
cal, don't you think? Miss Redmond?

A slight moment

Hallett You don't believe him.

Dee (*softly*) Yes.

Hallett Come on! Even you can't believe ...

Dee Yes! And so can you.

Stone I do see his problem. People don't behave like me, do they? Only in
plays. But *you*'re not a character in a play, Miss Redmond, you're only
too real. You sit down and you work out your plots ... so why shouldn't
I? It probably takes you what, a month? Two months? What if you had a
year, two years, six? Because that's what I've had.

Dee (*suddenly angry*) Because I'm not warped!

Stone You make fact into fiction. Why not turn fiction into fact? You
writers work out your plot and you try and fill in all the holes because
your audience is acting as the detective. Sorry, no, you don't fill in *all* the
holes because in the end, justice must be done, be seen to be done. You
have your murderer make a mistake. (*He takes up the pile of Acting
Editions*) But if I *read* your plots, if I fill in those holes—and after all,
you've shown me where they are ... I'm that much to the good, aren't I?
(*He smiles and drops the books back to their place*) You realize that I'm
trying to be very fair, giving you every chance to see the, er, the holes so
that you can fill them in for yourselves.

Dee I'll tell them exactly what's happened, I'll tell them everything you've
done ...

Stone Yes of course you will. I want you to. Which is why I want you to
hear exactly what I *have* done.

Dee No.

Hallett Listen to him, Dee.

Dee How can you *sit* there? Stand

Hallett I want to *know*.

Dee How much more is there to know? He's a madman, he's killed your
wife and all you do is ...

Stone Perhaps he'd like to know how I persuaded you to come here tonight?
Or perhaps you've already ...

Dee I've told him. I've *told* him!

Stone And presumably this is the story you'll tell his colleagues when they
ask.

Dee It's the truth, isn't it?

Stone That you came to see my wife? But my wife is dead ...

Dee You got me here with a pack of lies.

Stone So you say.

Dee Why else would I be here?

Stone What you'll say is that I persuaded you to come here with some cock-and-bull story about my invalid wife being an amateur purveyor of detective fiction who has sent a manuscript to you for your advice.

Dee Yes! Yes!

Stone But where is this wife? And where's the manuscript?

Dee (*looking round*) I brought it . . .

Stone And I took it. And didn't you say you couldn't find the letter she wrote to you?

A slight moment

Dee You took it—from my flat—you took it.

Stone It was under "General Correspondence". You really do have the most meticulous filing system.

Dee It would be in my diary.

Stone Sorry?

Dee Coming here. It's in my diary.

Stone Which is why I took that too. And destroyed it. Together with the letter and the manuscript. When you were alone here with Mr Hallett. So while of course you'll be able to *say* why you came here, proving why you came here might be a little more difficult.

A slight pause

Hallett And me?

Stone Much the same. In principle.

Hallett It's on record. In the book. "Meeting informant."

Stone (*feigning disappointment*) And you assured me that our first meeting would be strictly off the record.

Hallett You think I wouldn't cover myself?

Stone So it has been recorded.

Hallett (*lying*) That's right.

Stone "Meeting informant." Where? Here? No, on Wimbeldon Common.

Hallett And then here.

Stone Did that go in the book? Logged on your return?

Hallett says nothing

Even if it did, where's your proof? "Meeting informant"? Very vague, wouldn't you say? But a most convenient way of bumping up "the old expenses" and hardly ever queried, I should imagine. So it's your word against mine. And my word will be that the first time I saw you today was when you arrived here with your lady-friend.

A moment

Hallett So what I'm supposed to have done . . . is killed my wife . . .

Stone She having turned up unexpectedly at Miss Redmond's flat . . .

Hallett And then took a ride round here. Just for the hell of it.

Stone Not quite. You waited for Miss Redmond to return from her meeting. During which time you formulated the beginnings of your plan.

Hallett I already had a plan, did I?

Stone To put the blame on me.

Hallett Someone I haven't seen for six years.

Stone So you say.

Hallett Wadda *you* say?

Stone What *I* say is that, convinced of my guilt, you have been quietly waging a private war of nerves against me, trying to break me and thus secure your confession. That I finally did confess to the murder of my wife and child ... from which time you have been blackmailing me. You wouldn't be the first officer of the law tempted to take a shilling or two. I shall also say that on one occasion you came here, somewhat the worse for drink, with some half-baked proposal that I should kill your wife and thus give us both our freedom.

Hallett All of which you can prove, naturally.

Stone Again, it would be your word against mine. But I can provide evidence that you have visited me quite regularly.

Hallett (*spreading his hands*) ~~Please.~~ GO ON THEN

Stone Parking a car is difficult enough anywhere these days ... in a one-way street it's virtually impossible. (*Indicating the window*) Across the way there is a private block of flats. I once made the awesome mistake of parking in the forecourt whereupon the caretaker told me to "Piss off out of it before I phone the law." Do excuse me. You have a Ford ~~Cortina~~, ESCORT dark green, registration number VGH-five-seven-four-~~X~~. I have a Ford ~~Cortina~~ ESCORT, dark blue but hard to distinguish from green once the street lights are on. I also have a set of false numberplates. Had. If you telephone my local police station you will find that numerous complaints have been made about the illegal parking of a car, VGH-five-seven-four-~~R~~ Y. One such complaint was made earlier this evening.

Dee You would have been seen.

Stone Would I?

Dee Someone would have seen you, recognized you.

Stone What people remember—think they remember—is not the man, but the clothing. Wouldn't you say, Mr Hallett? Your average eye-witness? "A tall man in a brown jacket" ... "A short man in a bowler hat". So ... remove my glasses (*he does so*), put on a raincoat such as yours—(*he puts on Hallett's coat*)—~~C & A~~ MILLET'S, twenty-five pounds—and a hat such as yours— (*he puts on Hallett's hat*)—Dunn & Co., seven pounds fifty—and what is it your eye-witness will remember, if pressed? Odds on, the hat and coat and very little else. (*He removes the hat and coat*)

Hallett I could always say ... I could always prove ... that when I was supposed to be here ...

Stone I always chose a time when you were with your lady-friend. Whatever you told your wife or your colleagues on those occasions would have been a lie and thus to my convenience. Oh yes ... I quite often eat in a little restaurant round the corner in the High Street. On several occasions I have appeared rather depressed and once confided to my good friend the proprietor—Spiros, a Greek chappie—that I was "having trouble with the police". That I was being victimized. That my life wasn't my own. It's a sad comment on our times that he wasn't the least surprised at such a revelation. I quickly realized my mistake and begged him to keep the matter to himself. Which he no doubt will: unless asked to do otherwise. (*He takes the glasses and the ashtray from the coffe table and takes them into the kitchen*)

Hallett moves quickly to the phone and begins to dial

Dee What are you doing?
Hallett Waddaya think?
Dee *Tell* me.
Hallett Phoning her, waddaya think, I'm *phoning* her.
Stone (*coming out of the kitchen*) I've already said ...
Hallett Shut up! (*He listens, but the line is still engaged. He slowly replaces the receiver and rubs a hand across his mouth, unsure*)
Dee Why would you kill her?
Stone But you know why.
Dee (*forcing herself to keep calm*) Why ... why would we say you'd killed her ... what possible reason could we give ...
Stone Ah! What you say—and do try to remember this, it's very important—what you will say ... is exactly what has happened here this evening. That you were enveigled into coming here by a madman who has committed murder and, because of his hatred of you, has done everything I've said to have you charged with that murder. You are the innocent victims of a malignant mind. And once again ... it will be your word against mine. (*He takes the ice-bowl into the kitchen*)
Hallett I'm wrong. Yeah. I'm wrong. He really could have done it. He's that sick. (*He sits down slowly and looks at the palms of his hands, then up at Dee*) He could have killed her.
Dee What are we going to do?

Hallett doesn't react, but continues looking at her as Stone comes out of the kitchen

Stone By all means talk amongst yourselves.
Dee John ... what are we going to *do?*
Hallett (*confused*) I dunno. I ... I dunno.
Stone Even you, Mr Hallett, even you.
Dee Tell someone. Get them here.
Hallett I'll ... I'll go. That's better ... yeah ... I'll go ... on my own, see if I can ...
Stone Before you do—let me put you completely in the picture. My main purpose for getting you here this afternoon was to arrange your fingerprints on that knife and to persuade you to return this evening. I did this by means of a telephone call, supposedly from my wayward son. Perhaps Miss Redmond would like to explain this minor miracle of telecommunication? No? Later then. I also obtained one of your cigar butts which is now in an ashtray in Miss Redmond's flat. Also the button from your

coat. That was an unexpected bonus I must say. I took it when I hung up your coat in the lobby there. When you left, I went round to meet your wife as previously arranged. I persuaded her that perhaps we should arrive separately at the flat—I would go first and pave the way as it were. I knew from your diary that you would be at your meeting. I went into the flat and waited for her. Incidentally, whenever I went there I wore the raincoat and hat. And of course removed my glasses. While I waited, I changed my shirt. I noticed that you always wear the same shirts—either blue or white—Littlewoods, price three pounds ninety-nine. I was rather amused on one occasion to find two such shirts hanging in Miss Redmond's wardrobe. Two shirts and a pair of shoes. Hush Puppies. (*He opens the trunk and holds up a pair of shoes and a white shirt. He drops them back into the trunk*) Your wife arrived and—er—well, we won't dwell on those five minutes or so, will we. (*He lets the trunk lid fall*) I left, taking with me the knife and the shirt which was by now somewhat less than immaculate. Oh yes, I took them in one of your small holdalls, Miss Redmond. To Wimbledon Common as I said, using my car, with the false number plates. I returned here and waited for you. When I saw you arriving, I telephoned Mr Hallett as previously agreed. I knew it would take something like twenty minutes for you to get here: you took twenty-seven. When I saw you arriving, I made my excuse to leave and secreted myself on the landing upstairs until you came in. Once you were inside, I popped out and destroyed the manuscript and the papers. Which gave you time to poke around and deposit a fulsome collection of fingerprints. *I* always wore gloves. (*He smiles*) And here we are.

Pause

Dee And you really think you can get away with it.

Stone smiles and gives an open-handed gesture

The word of two totally innocent people against someone like you ... someone who's already been involved in murder ... someone with a mind like yours ...

Stone (*mockingly viciously*) "Two totally innocent people." Would you be here ... if you were totally innocent ...either of you? You used me ... to ply your dirty trade ... both of you. And now I'm using you. And even if I fail ... what does it matter? It'll never be the same for either of you. I've thrown the mud and the mud will stick against your wall just like it stuck against mine. You'll never be looked at the same ... never quite trusted, always the doubt. Both of you. The clever clever policeman and his little bit of stuff who writes fairy stories. (*He holds his smile of contempt and then, in the tone of someone trying to be helpful*) Incidentally, Miss Redmond ... one evening after he left you, I followed him to a pub where he met one of his colleagues. Their conversation was quite illuminating. Mr Hallett was describing how he was in "the clutches of a neurotic bitch who is beginning to make life hell for me". How he wished he could "get her off my back". How she was beginning to pressurize him, to make threats. All very well to have his little bit on the side ...

Hallett (*unconvincingly*) I never said that, any of it.
Dee No. (*She sounds as unconvincing as he did*)

Stone looks at his watch, and pushes the trunk back against the wall

Stone (*pleasantly*) I think you should go, don't you? My friend Spiros is
   coming round for a cup of coffee and a slice of honey-cake—nine
   o'clock—I'd hate for him to meet you. No doubt he'll still be here when
   your colleagues arrive to hear my side of the story. I hope so anyway, I'd
   like to have a witness.

*A moment. Hallett stands and his uncertainty seems to have gone, and been
replaced with an icy resolve*

Hallett I congratulate you. You've done a good job. You've really sewn it
   up nice and tight. So one way and another ... you've left me no alterna-
   tive. (*He takes up the knife, looks at it, then turns to Stone*)

Dee watches, afraid, as Hallett moves slowly towards Stone, holding the knife

A really nice little job of planting the evidence. You would have made a
   good copper. (*He is now close to Stone, the knife between them*) Mistake
   you made ... was trying to make a *fool* out of a good copper. (*He suddenly
   makes a thrust with the knife*)

*Stone throws up defensive arms as Dee moves forward instinctively to stop
Hallett, but suddenly Hallett stops*

(*To Dee*) All right, all right, you don't have to worry ... (*To Stone;
   mockingly arrogantly*) You berk. You stupid prissy little berk. (*He moves
   forward, prodding the knife at Stone*)

*Stone makes impotent little defensive gestures as he is driven back across the
room towards the bedroom wall*

You really think I'd forget *you?* A copper whose whole *game* is knowing
   faces? You think I didn't recognize you the minute you walked into
   that boozer? You berk ...
Stone Don't ... don't do that ...
Dee What are you saying ... (*She moves to grab Hallett's arm*) Tell me.

*Hallett shakes her off and prods the knife at Stone again, driving him across to
the other side of the room*

Hallett You think I didn't know something was up the minute you started
   following us around? You think I didn't know you were there? You see ...
   when you weren't following me ... I was following *you*. Because what I
   didn't know ... what I didn't know, sunshine ... was just exactly what
   your little game was.

Stone is now by the chair next to the drinks table

Dee You knew he was going to kill her ...
Hallett Kill her? Kill nothing. A pint of blood bought this morning from the

butcher for the garden and kept fresh in a thermos flask ... He's never been *near* her.

Dee The *telephone.*

Hallett Go on—tell her.

Hallett suddenly kicks out at the chair Stone is crouching next to. The chair knocks over the standard lamp, which goes out. Stone cowers on his hands and knees as Hallett stands threateningly over him

Stone Leave—me—alone.

Hallett Dodge they use in the motor trade, eh sunshine? Someone advertises a car cheap, dealer phones up, says he'll be round, they put the phone down, he doesn't ... leaves his off the hook and what happens, the line's engaged all the time, kosher punters can't get through ... (*With a sudden thrust of the knife*) Is that right?

Stone (*cowering*) Yes ... yes ...

Hallett He phoned my number from your flat, the wife answered, he left the phone off the hook ... (*He makes another thrust with the knife*) I went in after you and figured it out.

Dee You let me go through all this ...

Hallett No choice.

Dee You saw what he was doing to me ...

Hallett Use it in one of your stories.

Dee (*turning away*) You bastard ... you *bastard.*

Hallett I had to find out what his game was. Tell you and you'd blow the lot ... You can't get a tax demand without reaching for the Valium.

Dee You bastard ... you evil bastard ...

Hallett drags Stone to his feet and begins using the knife to back him away across the room again

Hallett Play games with *me*? I've been playing games with you ever since I came through that door. I'm a copper ... All coppers are actors, didn't you know sunshine? I could *cry* if it got me what I wanted ...

Stone is now at the bedroom door. He suddenly opens the door and tries to get inside and close the door behind him, but Hallett knocks the door back, grabs Stone and shoves him backwards into the bedroom. The Lights come up on the bedroom

Dee Leave him.

Hallett hurls Stone down on to his knees by the bed

Hallett You know what really got up my nose about you those six years ago? You know what really made me give you a bad time? Your self-pity ... your whining self-pity ... All you ever talked about was you, what it was doing to *you* ... Your wife and kid get butchered and all you can think about is what it will do to *you.*

Dee (*moving towards the bedroom*) Leave him!

Hallett takes up the balloon-face and thrusts it close against Stone's face

Hallett You think I didn't recognize her? Your wife? You think I'd ever
forget that face ... the face of that kid ...? (*Suddenly he bursts the balloon
with the knife*)

Dee turns away and moves from the bedroom door

Why did the marriage break up? Why did she divorce you? Why did she
want you out of the house? Because she couldn't stand the sight of you
and you knew it ... You with your sorry this and your sorry that ... You
make me vomit. (*His face is twisted in utter contempt. He moves to the
doorway, but turns*) You'd been any sort of man and they'd be alive today
and that's what you know, that's what you can't stand, isn't it, sunshine ...
And because you're so bloody pathetic you have to try and put the blame
on someone else. Well they're dead ... and they're dead because of *you*.
(*He moves away, contemptuously tossing the knife down on to the sofa and
moving behind the sofa to pull on his raincoat, his back to the bedroom*)

Stone, kneeling, hands to face, down by the bed, suddenly lets out a great cry

Stone No ...!

*Stone moves quickly into the sitting-room, snatches up the knife and makes to
attack Hallett, who is caught with one arm inside his coat. Dee screams as the
two men grapple behind the sofa, knocking over the desk lamp, which goes out.
Hallett finally gets the knife from Stone and punches him in the stomach.
Stone doubles up as Hallett moves back against the wall, running the back of
his hand against his mouth, still holding the knife*

Hallett (*breathlessly*) All right ... that's enough ...

*Stone suddenly lunges at Hallett with his hands to his throat, forcing him back
against the wall. Hallett tries to release Stone's grip with his free hand. Stone
now has one hand at Hallett's throat and is using the other to seize Hallett's
wrist, slowly turning the knife upwards and towards himself. A moment. Hallett is unable to move back because of the wall. Suddenly Stone wins the trial of
strength, and pulls the knife into his own stomach*

Jesus Christ!

*Stone releases his grip and moves backwards, so that the knife is left in
Hallett's hand, with Hallett and Dee staring at it. Stone, his shoulders heaving
with the effort of breathing, drops to his knees, both his hands to his stomach
from which blood is beginning to seep. Hallett looks down at Stone, who for all
the pain, looks back in cold triumph*

I'll—I'll get an ambulance. (*He moves to the telephone but then turns
to Dee and then, suddenly, angrily*) He pulled me ... he pulled me on to
himself

The doorbell rings. It doesn't seem to register

Dee (*flatly*) It's what he wanted ... Can't you see ... the three of us ...
finished.

Stone Well done, Miss ... (*But he is unable to finish*)

Dee (*moving to Hallett; coldly*) Help him. (*Suddenly very calm, she takes the receiver from Hallett*) I'll phone. You help him. (*More firmly*) Help him.

But Hallett can only stand looking impotently at Stone who is trying to lever himself to his feet by the corner of the sofa. The doorbell rings

Stone My ... friend ... Spiros. Do let him in, Miss ... (*He falls, chest heaving*)

Dee begins to dial. And Hallett remains staring down at Stone. And the ringing at the door begins again, persistently, as the Lights slowly fade to a Black-out, and—

the CURTAIN *falls*

FURNITURE AND PROPERTY LIST

ACT I

SCENE 1

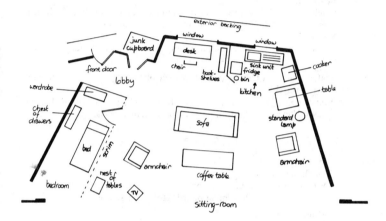

On stage: **Sitting-room:**

Sofa. *On it:* cushions

2 armchairs

Coffee table. *On it:* tray bearing plate with remains of egg and bacon
meal and dirty knife and fork, 2 empty cans of beer, empty crumpled
cigarette packet, breadboard with remains of a loaf and a carving knife

Table

Desk. *On it:* desk lamp. *In drawer:* pair of thin gloves, bundle of papers

Chair

Bookshelves. *On them:* a few books

Nest of small tables

TV set

On floor by settee: filthy ashtray, newspaper, telephone, telephone directory

Carpet

Window curtains (open)

Lobby:

Coathooks by front door (unseen)

In junk cupboard: battered old railway trunk with new padlock. *In trunk:*
holdall containing black plastic bin-bag, raincoat and hat identical to
those worn by Hallett (*for ACT I, Scene 1*); plastic bag for blood-
stained rubber gloves (*for ACT I, Scene 2*); blood-stained embroidered
hotel towel rolled up in plastic, pair of Hush Puppies shoes, white shirt,
carving knife wrapped in plastic bag (*for ACT II*)

Kitchen:
Sink and taps (practical)
Draining-board. *In drawer underneath:* 2 plastic freezer bags
Refrigerator (practical). *In it:* vacuum flask, bowl of ice
Cooker
Pedal bin
Tea-towel on hook by sink
Venetian blind (open)
Other dressing as space allows

Bedroom:
Single bed with bedclothes. *In it:* dummy made of pillows, with head
    made from a balloon with photograph of woman stuck on it and wig
Wardrobe
Chest of drawers. *On it:* small empty pill-bottle (*for* **Stone** *in ACT I,*
    Scene 2)

Personal: **Hallett:** coins in trouser pocket, packet of thin cigars, box of matches,
    wrist-watch
    Stone: spectacles; *in jacket pockets:* handkerchief, typewritten checklist,
    set of keys, coat-button, lighter; loose change, wallet (*for ACT II*)

SCENE 2

Strike: Newspaper
    Telephone directory
    Dirty ashtray from kitchen sink
    Tray with dirty dishes, breadboard, etc., from kitchen

Set: **Sitting-room:**
    Trunk in centre of room with lid open
    On coffee table: glass of sherry, clean ashtray, pile of six French's Acting
        Editions
    On table by kitchen: bowl of flowers, small glasses, bottles of whisky,
        vodka, sherry and tonic, dish of lemon slices
    Portable typewriter with cover on desk
    Knitting and needles on armchair DR
    On bookshelves: vase, more books, a few plants
    Stone's jacket over back of sofa
    Window curtains closed

    Kitchen:
    Water in sink
    On draining board: freshly washed crockery (2 cups, saucers, plates, etc.),
        upturned vacuum flask
    Venetian blind closed

Off stage: A4 envelope (open, addressed and stamped) containing script **(Dee)**

Personal: **Stone:** blood-stained rubber gloves; key wrapped in handkerchief, wrist-
    watch in cardigan pocket
    Dee: wrist-watch, shoulder-bag containing cigarettes and lighter

ACT II

Set: **Hallett's** hat and coat on armchair DL

LIGHTING PLOT

Practical fittings required: wall-brackets, desk lamp, standard lamp, television, pendant in lobby, pendant in bedroom, pendant in kitchen, refrigerator in kitchen

Interior. A first-floor flat. The same scene throughout

ACT I SCENE 1   Afternoon

To open: General effect of an autumn afternoon. Wall-brackets on, kitchen light on, TV effect on

Cue 1	**Stone** switches off TV set *Fade TV effect*	(Page 2)
Cue 2	**Stone** switches off kitchen light *Snap off kitchen light*	(Page 11)
Cue 3	**Stone** switches off sitting-room light *Snap off wall-brackets*	(Page 11)
Cue 4	**Stone** exits *Slow fade to Black-out*	(Page 11)

ACT I SCENE 2   Evening

To open: Wall-brackets on, desk lamp on, TV effect on, kitchen light on

Cue 5	**Stone** switches on standard lamp *Snap on standard lamp*	(Page 11)
Cue 6	**Stone** switches on lobby light *Snap on light in lobby*	(Page 12)
Cue 7	**Stone** switches off TV set *Fade TV effect*	(Page 12)
Cue 8	**Dee** taps gently at bedroom door *Bring up lights on bedroom*	(Page 23)
Cue 9	**Dee** sits on settee staring at the empty pill bottle *Slow fade to Black-out*	(Page 24)

ACT II   Evening

To open: Wall-brackets on, desk lamp on, standard lamp on, kitchen light on, lobby light on

Cue 10	**Hallett** knocks over chair and standard lamp *Snap off standard lamp*	(Page 50)
Cue 11	**Hallett** shoves **Stone** backwards into bedroom *Bring up lights on bedroom*	(Page 50)
Cue 12	**Hallett** and **Stone** grapple, knocking over desk lamp *Snap off desk lamp*	(Page 51)
Cue 13	Doorbell rings persistently *Slow fade to Black-out*	(Page 52)

EFFECTS PLOT

ACT I

SCENE 1

Cue 1   As CURTAIN rises   (Page 1)
           Low racing commentary from TV

Cue 2   **Stone** turns off TV   (Page 2)
           Snap off TV commentary

Cue 3   **Stone** replaces receiver and moves away from telephone   (Page 8)
           Pause, then telephone rings

SCENE 2

Cue 4   As CURTAIN rises   (Page 11)
           Low sound from TV

Cue 5   **Stone** replaces receiver   (Page 12)
           Pause, then doorbell rings

Cue 6   **Stone** turns off TV   (Page 12)
           Snap off TV sound

Cue 7   **Stone:** "... and the telephone rings."   (Page 18)
           Telephone rings

Cue 8   **Dee:** "... Are you all right? Mrs Stone?"   (Page 23)
           Doorbell rings

ACT II

Cue 9   **Hallett:** "... at least *I* will."   (Page 26)
           Pause, then sound of key in front door

Cue 10   **Hallett:** "... he pulled me on to him ..."   (Page 51)
           Doorbell rings

Cue 11   **Dee:** "... Help him."   (Page 52)
           Pause, then doorbell rings

Cue 12   **Dee** begins to dial   (Page 52)
           Doorbell rings persistently; continue until
           CURTAIN *is down*

MADE AND PRINTED IN GREAT BRITAIN BY
LATIMER TREND & COMPANY LTD PLYMOUTH

MADE IN ENGLAND

APRIL 18·19 W/Th.

MAY 2/3/4 W/Th/F

Then every Wed/Thu